DANGEROUS WEATHER

BLIZZARDS

Michael Allaby

☑®

Facts On File, Inc.

Blizzards

Facts On File, Inc.
11 Penn Plaza
New York NY 10001

Library of Congress Cataloging-in-Publication Data

Allaby, Michael.
    Blizzards / Michael Allaby.
        p.   cm. — (Dangerous weather)
    Includes index.
    ISBN 0-8160-3518-0 (alk. paper)
    1. Blizzards.   I. Title.   II. Series: Allaby, Michael. Dangerous
weather.
    QC926.32.A45   1997
    551.55′5—dc21   96-49207

Facts On File books are available at special discounts when purchased in bulk quantities for businesses, associations, institutions or sales promotions. Please call our Special Sales Department in New York at (212) 967-8800 or (800) 322-8755.

Text design by Richard Garratt
Cover design by Matt Galemmo
Illustrations by Richard Garratt

Printed in the United States of America

RRD FOF 10 9 8 7 6 5 4 3 2 1

Table of Contents

What is a blizzard?

Wherever he goes in public, the president of the United States is followed by journalists eager to overhear a chance remark or photograph an unguarded move or expression. The president expects this, but on January 7, 1996, President and Mrs. Clinton escaped, at least for a while. It was a Sunday morning and they were going to the morning service at St. John's Church, not far from the White House. What made that morning different was the snow. Well wrapped up against the cold, the Clintons trudged through drifts. The journalists, trying to follow in a press van, got stuck and were left behind.

Along with much of the Appalachian and mid-Atlantic states, Washington was deep in snow that morning after the worst blizzard in 70 years. In South Carolina, university students played in the snow, and a man jogging near the White House described it as "gorgeous, spectacular, almost awe-inspiring." For most people, though, the blizzards caused huge disruption, and there were at least 65 deaths. In New York City mail deliveries were halted and there were 20-foot drifts at the airports. The United Nations closed. People traveled to work on skis across Times Square. In parts of

Figure 1: *Car parked on a street in Philadelphia is buried in snow after a blizzard in January, 1996.* (Courtesy of Chandra Speeth, 1996)

Virginia and eastern Tennessee drifts were 30 feet deep; they were 24 feet deep in eastern Kentucky, and there was a foot of snow even in northeastern Georgia. Shenandoah National Park, Virginia, lay under almost four feet of snow. The blizzard affected 17 states, and states of emergency were declared in nine.

For Sunday night, the National Weather Service forecast between 20 and 30 inches of snow driven into drifts by winds of 25 to 35 MPH. Those were the forecast speeds for steady winds, however, and at times there were gusts of up to 50 MPH as the storm traveled north and east, before eventually moving over the Atlantic.

Hardly had people begun clearing away the snow before new storms developed and brought more, bringing the death toll to more than 100. In Washington, federal government offices had managed to reopen on Thursday, but were closed again on Friday. By this time the weight of snow was causing damage. A church roof collapsed in Harlem; a supermarket roof collapsed in North Massapequa, New York; a lawn and garden center and a barn collapsed in Pennsylvania; and the roof of a store collapsed in Ontario, Ohio. At Dale City, Virginia, Potomac Mills Mall, one of the biggest shopping malls in the country, had to be closed for a day because the roof was sagging under the weight of snow.

Blizzard is a word we tend to associate with the far north or with Antarctica. Certainly blizzards are more common there. While all was quiet in Washington that Sunday morning, a Norwegian tourist gazing at the White House said the weather was "quite normal." As this example demonstrates, however, blizzards also happen in lower latitudes and with much more serious consequences. The population is sparsely scattered in northern Scandinavia, Siberia, and northern Canada, and no one at all lives permanently in Antarctica. The eastern United States is much more densely populated and ordinary life requires transportation systems, telephone lines, and power supplies, all of which can be disrupted by heavy snow, and the damage to property is often costly. Insurance claims following the 1996 blizzards were estimated at about $585 million.

As America recovered, Britain began to suffer. Blizzards began there early in February. More than 1,000 motorists spent 22 hours stranded in southern Scotland on one of the main roads into the country from the south. In South Wales thousands of homes lost their electricity. Blocked roads meant 2,000 workers had to spend the night at the nuclear reprocessing plant at Sellafield, in northwest England, and by the second night 1,000 of them still could not return home. The blizzards continued intermittently for several weeks, blocking roads and bringing down power lines. They even closed Scottish ski resorts. Ferries stayed in port, and North Sea oil rigs were isolated when winds of more than 100 MPH grounded the helicopters that carry supplies to them and ferry workers back and forth.

A blizzard is not merely snow, it is snow driven by high winds. It is not even necessary for snow to be falling. Blizzards can occur when light, powdery snow lying on the ground is blown into the air, like a desert dust storm. The word itself is American and the first record of its use dates from 1829. It may have come from *blizzer* or *blizzom*, adjectives meaning *dazzling* or *blazing*. In the Civil War a heavy volley of musket fire was called a blizzard and in 1870 an Indiana newspaper used it to describe a ferocious snowstorm. That usage caught on and within 10 years or so it became the only meaning of the word. Today, the National Oceanic and Atmospheric Administration defines a blizzard as a storm with winds of at least 35 MPH, temperatures lower than 20° F, and enough falling or blowing snow to reduce visibility to less than a quarter of a mile.

Continental and maritime climates

A blizzard consists of wind-driven snow. Strong winds can occur anywhere, but two conditions are needed to produce snow. There must be ample water vapor in the air to condense and fall to the ground, and the air temperature near the ground must be low enough to prevent the water from melting after it has left the cloud from which it falls. Not everywhere in the world has a climate moist enough for this to happen, and not everywhere is cold enough.

All our weather, blizzards included, results from solar radiation and its indirect effect on the air. Warmth from the Sun heats the ground and the surface of the sea and these warm the air in contact with them. When air is warmed, it expands. This makes it less dense, so it rises and as it rises it cools again. This is called *adiabatic* cooling (see box on page 4) and if air is made to descend it warms in the same way. The amount of water vapor air can hold depends on the temperature. As air cools, its water vapor condenses and clouds form. As air warms, water evaporates into it.

If this is all there were to it, the weather would be easy to understand, but rather boring. It would not change much from one day to the next and certainly not from one time of year to another. There would be no seasons.

We have seasons because the Earth is tilted on its axis. As it travels through its orbit about the Sun, first the northern hemisphere and then the southern is tilted toward the Sun. As figure 2 shows, this alters the amount of sunshine each hemisphere receives, not only in intensity but also in duration. Summer days are longer than winter days and the Arctic and Antarctic Circles mark the boundary of regions where on at least one day in winter the Sun never rises

Adiabatic warming and cooling

Air is compressed by the weight of air above it. Imagine a balloon partly inflated with air and made from some substance that totally insulates the air inside. No matter what the temperature outside the balloon, the temperature of the air inside remains the same.

Imagine the balloon is released into the atmosphere. The air inside is squeezed between the weight of air above it, all the way to the top of the atmosphere, and the denser air below it.

Suppose the air inside the balloon is less dense than the air above it. The balloon will rise. As it rises, the distance to the top of the atmosphere becomes smaller, so there is less air above to weigh down on the air in the balloon. At the same time, as it moves through air that is less dense, it experiences less pressure from below. This causes the air in the balloon to expand.

When air (or any gas) expands, its molecules move further apart. The *amount* of air remains the same, but it occupies a bigger volume. As they move apart, the molecules must "push" other molecules out of their way. This uses energy, so as the air expands its molecules lose energy. Because they have less energy they move more slowly.

When a moving molecule strikes something, some of its energy of motion (kinetic energy) is transferred to whatever it strikes and part of that energy is converted into heat. This raises the temperature of the struck object by an amount related to the number of molecules striking it and their speed.

In expanding air, the molecules are moving further apart, so a smaller number of them strike an object each second. They are also traveling more slowly, so they strike with less force. This means the temperature of the air decreases. As it expands, air cools.

If the air in the balloon is denser than the air below, it will descend. The pressure on it will increase, its volume will decrease, and its molecules will acquire more energy. Its temperature will increase.

This warming and cooling has nothing to do with the temperature of the air surrounding the balloon. It is called *adiabatic* warming and cooling, from the Greek word *adiabatos*, meaning impassable.

You can easily demonstrate adiabatic cooling and warming for yourself with experiment 1 in *A Chronology of Weather*.

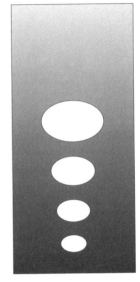

Effect of air pressure on rising and sinking air.

above the horizon and on one day in summer it never sinks below the horizon. At the other extreme, the Tropics of Capricorn and Cancer mark the limits of regions where on at least one day every year the Sun is directly overhead at noon.

Even if the Earth were not tilted, the poles would still be colder than the tropics. In fact, they would be colder than they are now, because in summer the tilted axis turns them toward the Sun. They are colder because the light and heat the surface receives is spread over a larger area when the Sun is low in the sky than when it is high, so it is less intense. This is something you can easily demonstrate (see experiment 13 in *A Chronology of Weather*).

On the Moon, which is close to Earth and receives much the same amount of solar radiation for each square mile of its surface, conditions are extreme. In areas illuminated by the Sun equatorial temperatures reach about 230° F, and in the dark areas they fall to about -274° F. Unlike the Moon, Earth has an atmosphere and oceans and these are what make the difference. Without them, the Earth would be as hot and as cold as the Moon. As it is, the lowest temperature ever recorded at ground level was -126.9° F, in Antarctica, and the highest was 136° F, in Libya. Air and sea water, warmed in the tropics, move into higher latitudes and their place is taken by colder air and water moving toward the equator. This constant movement transfers heat from low latitudes to high latitudes, warming cold regions, cooling warm regions, and making climates much more uniform than they would be otherwise. The difference between extreme temperatures on the Moon is 504° F and on Earth 264° F. On Earth such extremes of cold and heat are unusual and very local, but on the Moon they are common and widespread, so the real difference between the two bodies is much greater than the numbers indicate.

Figure 2: *How axial tilt produces the seasons.*

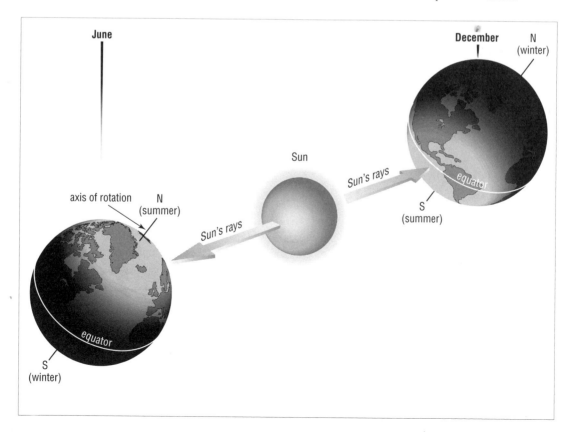

Global circulation of the atmosphere

The tropics, of Cancer in the north and Capricorn in the south, mark the boundaries of the belt around the Earth where the Sun is directly overhead at noon on at least one day in the year. The Arctic and Antarctic Circles mark the boundaries of regions in which the Sun does not rise above the horizon on at least one day of the year and does not sink below the horizon on at least one day in the year.

Imagine a beam of sunlight just a few degrees wide. As the drawing shows, this beam illuminates a much smaller area if the Sun is directly overhead than it does if the Sun is at a low angle in the sky. The amount of energy

Global distribution of pressure.

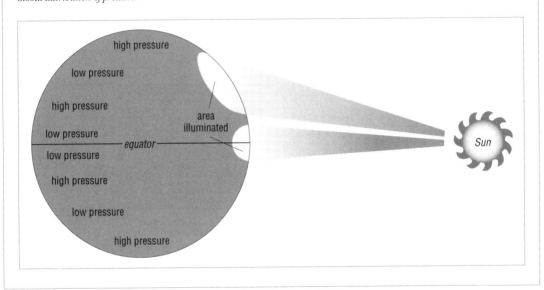

Uneven heating of the Earth sets the air in motion. In the lower part of the atmosphere, called the *troposphere*, this produces a general atmospheric circulation (see above). Air moves vertically as well as horizontally and there are belts around the world where dense air is usually sinking, making the surface pressure high, and other belts where less dense air is rising and surface pressure is low.

This global circulation of air is the first ingredient in the making of our weather. The oceans are the second. They warm and cool much more slowly than the land (see box on page 83). In summer, the land heats rapidly and the air above it becomes very warm. If that air moves away from the land and over the ocean, it will be cooled. In winter the opposite occurs. The land cools faster than the ocean and air moving from land to sea is warmed.

Ocean water is not at the same temperature everywhere, however, because it is also transporting heat. It does so as currents, some carrying warm water away from the equator, others carrying cool in each beam is the same because they are of the same width, so energy is spread over a smaller area directly beneath the Sun than it is when the Sun is lower. This is why the tropics are heated more strongly than any other part of the Earth and the amount of heat we receive from the Sun decreases the further we are from the equator.

Solar energy warms the surface of land and water. The air is warmed by contact with the surface. As it is warmed, the air expands. This makes it less dense than the air immediately above it, so it rises, its place near the surface being taken by denser air flowing inward. This air is heated in its turn.

Where the surface is heated strongly and air in contact with it is expanding, there will be a region of low surface atmospheric pressure. The equatorial belt is a region of generally low pressure.

At high altitude, the rising air cools, becomes more dense, and sinks. Where the sinking air reaches the surface the atmospheric pressure will be high. The edges of the tropics and the subtropics, where equatorial air is sinking, are regions of generally high pressure, one in each hemisphere. Although the air is very cold while it remains at a great height, as it sinks and is compressed it warms adiabatically (without mixing with surrounding air), so air in the tropical-subtropical regions is warm.

Over the poles, very cold air sinks to the surface. This produces generally high pressure.

Between the low-latitude high pressure and the high-latitude high pressure there is, in each hemisphere, a belt of generally low pressure.

Air movements carry warm air away from the tropics and cool air away from polar regions. This distributes the warmth we receive from the Sun more evenly than would be possible if the Earth had no atmosphere.

Although the Earth is heated most strongly in the tropics, all parts of the planet receive some warmth from the Sun, and land and water respond differently. Land warms and cools much faster than water. As air moves, it is warmed or cooled by the surface over which it travels.

Together, the transport of heat from low to high latitudes and the difference in the effect of heating on land and water generate the global circulation of the atmosphere. It is this circulation that produces regional climates and our day-to-day weather.

water away from the poles. In the large oceans these currents form *gyres*, roughly circular systems of currents which flow counterclockwise in both hemispheres. In the North Atlantic, water flowing eastward just north of the equator as the North Equatorial Current changes its name to the Antilles Current in the Caribbean and turns north when it reaches North America, flowing along the United States coast as the Florida Current and then the Gulf Stream. It turns east at about the latitude of Nova Scotia, where it meets the Labrador Current, bringing cold water southward on the western side of the sea between Canada and Greenland (water flows north along the west coast of Greenland, forming another counterclockwise gyre). In about the latitude of Spain the Gulf Stream turns south again, toward the equator, but part of it breaks away to flow past the British Isles and along the west coast of Norway. Still a warm current, this is called the North Atlantic Drift. The system of Atlantic currents is illustrated in figure 3.

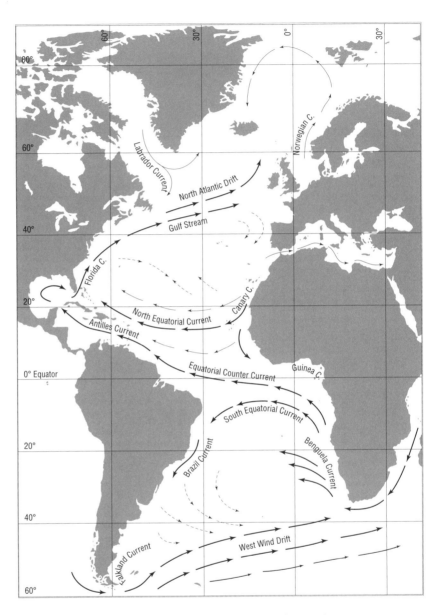

Figure 3: *Atlantic Ocean currents.*

The North Pacific gyre brings cool water down the western coast of North America as the California Current. Similar gyres occur in the South Pacific, South Atlantic, and Indian Oceans. In each case, the gyres bathe western coasts with warm water and eastern coasts with cool water. This means the eastern coastal regions of continents have a cooler climate than those on the west coast.

Along all coasts, climates are strongly affected by the ocean nearby. They are said to be *maritime*. Precipitation (rain and snow) is spread fairly evenly through the year. In New York City, for example, there is no month with no precipitation: based on an average of 46 years, the amount each month ranges from a minimum of 3.0 inches in November to a maximum of 4.3 inches in August. In Belfast, Northern Ireland, the driest month is April, with an average over 30 years of 1.9 inches of precipitation, and the wettest July, with 3.7 inches. Average temperatures are also fairly equable, in New York ranging from a daytime minimum of 37° F in January to a maximum of 82° F in July. In Belfast the average daytime temperature reaches 43° F in January and 65° F in July and August.

Deep inside continents the climate is drier because of the great distance to the moist air of the oceans. It is also hotter in summer and colder in winter because the oceans have a much smaller moderating effect on temperatures. At Omaha, Nebraska, in about the same latitude as New York, January is the driest month, with an average of 0.7 inch of precipitation, and June the wettest, with 4.6 inches. Average daytime temperatures range from 30° F in January to 86° F in July. The temperature difference between the warmest and coolest months is 45° F in New York and 56° F in Omaha. In Berlin, about 2° south of Belfast, March is the driest month, with 1.3 inches of precipitation, and July the wettest, with 2.9 inches. In January the average daytime temperature is 35° F and in July it is

Figure 4: *Main climate types.*

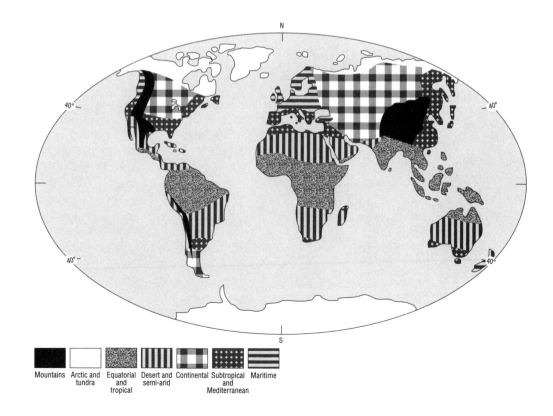

75° F. This gives Belfast a temperature range of 22° F and Berlin one of 40° F. These rather dry climates with greater ranges of temperature are called *continental.*

Most middle latitude climates are of either the maritime or continental type, with some being transitional between the two. These, mainly in north-central Europe, sometimes resemble maritime and other times continental climates.

As figure 4 shows, the middle-latitude climates are bordered to the north by subarctic (with tundra vegetation) and Arctic climates (no southern-hemisphere continent extends far enough south to have a subarctic climate). On the side nearer the equator, middle-latitude climates give way to subtropical and Mediterranean climates, then to desert and semiarid climates, and then to tropical and equatorial climates.

It is only in the middle latitudes that climates are both moist and cold enough in winter for blizzards to occur. Subarctic and Arctic climates also experience blizzards, but these are mainly of blowing, not falling snow (see page 31).

Movements of air masses in winter

Regions of the Earth have particular types of climate, but it is the air that produces climate. It might be more accurate to think of particular kinds of air, rather than geographical regions, as being associated with climates. After all, clouds form in air, not on the ground, and it is the movement of air that we feel as the wind. If one area is desert and in another it rains almost perpetually, there must be differences in the air over them.

It may seem strange to think of different kinds of air. After all, air is the same everywhere. It is dustier or more polluted in some places than others, but if you ignore the pollutants, all air is the same mixture of gases, about 78% nitrogen and 21% oxygen, with trace amounts of carbon dioxide, neon, helium, methane, and about five others. Go to the South Pole, the middle of the Sahara, a South Pacific island, or anywhere else you choose, and this is the air you will breathe (which is just as well if you are planning a trip!).

Ask a chemist to describe the air and this is the sort of answer you will receive, and it is perfectly true as far as it goes. All the same, the air may not *feel* the same everywhere or in the same place all the time. Sometimes it feels fresh and clean, at other times heavy and oppressive. These are real differences, so something must cause them.

Think of what it is like in the middle of a large continent in midwinter. The ground cooled rapidly in the fall, and now it is extremely cold. Lakes and rivers are frozen over. Air in contact with the surface is at the same temperature as the surface, and it is dry. Any water on the ground is frozen, so it cannot evaporate, and the amount of water vapor that air can hold decreases as the air temperature falls. Between 95° F and -23° F the amount of water vapor that air can hold decreases by half for every 18° F decrease in temperature. Even if liquid water were available, therefore, very little of it could evaporate. Step outdoors here and the air will feel clean and fresh.

When air is cold its molecules have less energy. They move more slowly and crowd closer together, so a given weight of cold air occupies a smaller volume than the same weight of warm air. This is something you can prove for yourself (see experiment 4 in *A Chronology of Weather*). If the molecules are more tightly crowded together in cold than in warm air, the cold air must be denser. Crowding together leaves no gaps, however. There are no places left without any air because the air has shrunk. Instead, air is drawn down from above and replaced with air flowing into the region at a high altitude. This means a column of air stretching from an area of the surface all the way to the top of the atmosphere contains more air molecules when the air is cold than it does when the air is warm. Because it contains more molecules, it is heavier, and because it is heavier it presses downward more strongly. In other words, its pressure increases at the surface.

Continents are large and so this cold, dense, dry air covers many thousands of square miles and throughout that area all the air is at more or less the same temperature, surface pressure, and contains the same amount of moisture. These shared characteristics also extend vertically. This body of air over the continental interior is called a *continental air mass* (see box on page 12) and it determines the type of weather people on the ground experience.

Air masses also form over the ocean and are called *maritime air masses*. They are different from continental air masses. Although in winter they are cold, they are not so cold as continental air masses in the same latitude, because the oceans cool much more slowly than the land. In midwinter the sea is warmer than the air above it. You can check this for yourself if you live near the coast and your local TV weather forecasts give the sea temperature as well as the air temperature. Maritime air is also moister than continental air, partly because it is warmer and can hold more water vapor but mainly because it is in contact with liquid water. Maritime air produces milder, wetter weather than continental air. Warm, very moist air can feel oppressive.

This makes it sound as though air just sits over a continent or ocean, producing typical climates. Climates are typical, but air masses are constantly on the move. They form, not in stationary air, but in air that is moving all the time, and they acquire their

Air masses and the weather they bring

As air moves slowly across the surface it is sometimes warmed, sometimes cooled; in some places water evaporates into it, and in others it loses moisture. Its characteristics change.

When it crosses a very large region, such as a continent or ocean, its principal characteristics are evened out and over a vast area all the air is at much the same temperature and pressure and is equally moist or dry. Such a body of air is called an *air mass*.

Air masses are warm, cool, moist, or dry according to the region over which they formed and are named accordingly. The names and their abbreviations are straightforward. Continental (c) air masses form over continents, maritime (m) ones over oceans. Depending on the latitude in which they form, air masses may be Arctic (A), polar (P), tropical (T), or equatorial (E). Except in the case of equatorial air, these categories are then combined to give continental Arctic (cA), maritime Arctic (mA), continental

polar (cP), maritime polar (mP), continental tropical (cT), and maritime tropical (mT).

North America is affected by mP, cP, cT, and mT air, the maritime air masses originating over the Pacific, Atlantic, or Gulf. As they move from where they formed (called their *source regions*) air masses change, but they do so slowly and at first they bring with them the weather conditions that produced them. As their names suggest, maritime air is moist, continental air is dry, polar air is cool, and tropical air is warm. At the surface there is little difference between polar and Arctic air, but there are differences in the upper atmosphere.

It is cP air spilling south when the cT and mT move toward the equator in the fall that brings cold, dry winters to the central United States. It is the meeting of mT air from the Gulf and cT air from inland that produces fierce storms in the south-east of the country.

Air masses affecting North America.

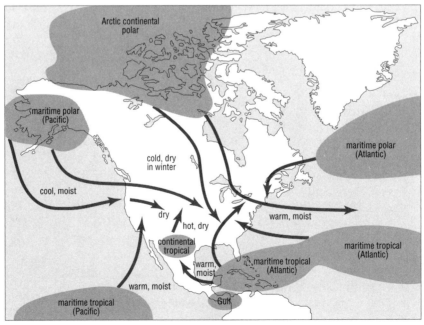

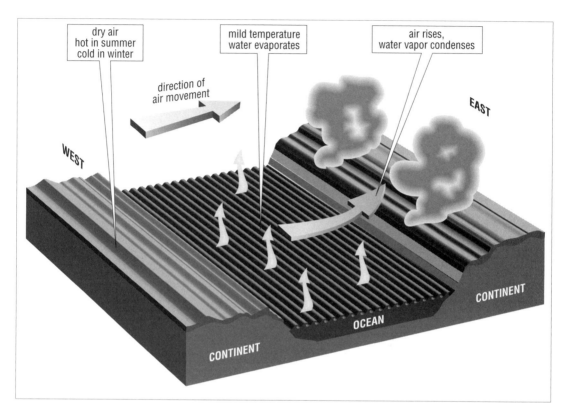

characteristics because of the great distances they must travel. In middle latitudes, air moves mainly from west to east, which is the direction of the prevailing winds. To either side of these latitudes winds generally blow in the opposite direction, from east to west. This can complicate weather forecasting in regions close to the boundaries. Over the world as a whole, equal amounts of air move from west to east and from east to west (if more air moved in one direction than in the other, friction between it and the surface would accelerate or decelerate the rotation of the Earth; the rate of rotation remains constant, so we can be sure the easterly and westerly winds balance).

Pacific air gives the west coast of North America a maritime climate. Portland, Oregon, for example, has maximum daytime temperatures ranging over 33° F, from 44° F in January to 77° F in July and August and precipitation falls in all months, although July and August are the driest. Continuing its passage over the continent, the air must travel more than 2,000 miles before reaching the Atlantic. During this time it loses much of its moisture and becomes continental in character. By the time it reaches Minneapolis it is much drier and brings temperatures ranging through 61° F, from 22° F in January to 83° F in July. The maritime air mass from the Pacific has become a continental air mass. Then it crosses the east

Figure 5: *Change in air mass as it crosses the ocean.*

Weather fronts

During the First World War, the Norwegian meteorologist Vilhelm Bjerknes (see *A Chronology of Weather* for biographical details) discovered that air forms distinct masses. Because each mass differs in its average temperature, and therefore density, from adjacent

Frontal depressions.

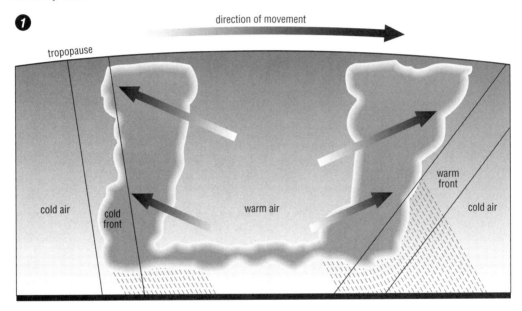

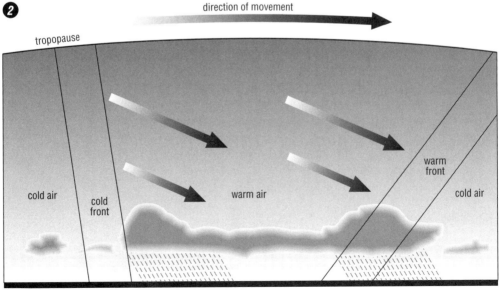

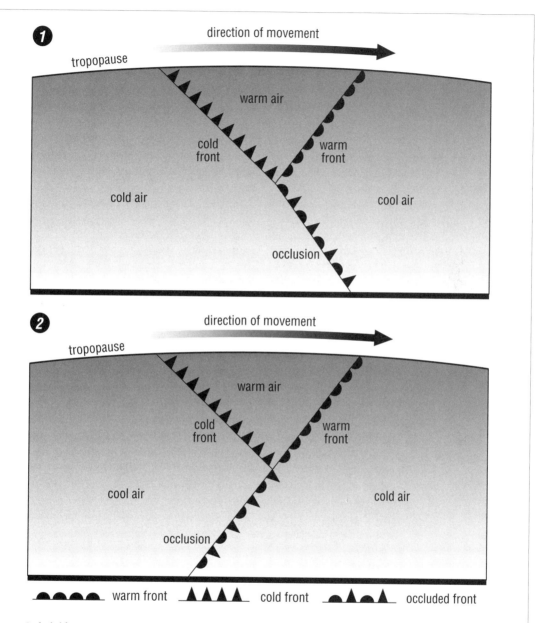

Occluded fronts.

masses, air masses do not mix readily. He called the boundary between two air masses a *front*.

Air masses move across the surface of land and sea, and so the fronts between them also move. Fronts are named according to the tem- perature of the air *behind* the front compared with that ahead of it. If the air behind the advancing front is warmer than the air ahead of it, it is a *warm front*. If the air behind the front is cooler, it is a *cold front*.

Fronts extend from the surface all the way to the tropopause, which is the boundary between the lower (troposphere) and upper (stratosphere) layers of the atmosphere. They slope upward, like the sides of a bowl, but the slope is very shallow. Warm fronts have a gradient of 1° or less, cold fronts of about 2°.

Cold fronts usually move faster across the surface of land and sea than warm fronts, so cold air trends to undercut warm air, raising it upward along the edge of the cold front. If warm air is rising, it will be raised even faster along the front separating it from cold air. The cold front is then called an *ana-front* and there is usually thick cloud and heavy rain or snow. If the warm air is sinking, an advancing cold front will raise it less. This is a *kata-front*, usually with only low-level cloud and light rain, drizzle, or fine snow.

After a front has formed, waves start to develop along it. These are shown on weather maps and as they become steeper, areas of low pressure form at their crests. These are *frontal depressions*, which often bring wet weather. Just below the wave crest, there is cold air to either side of a body of warm air. The cold front moves faster than the warm front, lifting the warm air along both fronts until all the warm air is clear of the surface. The fronts are then said to be *occluded* and the pattern they form is called an *occlusion*.

Once the fronts are occluded and the warm air is no longer in contact with the surface, air to both sides of the occlusion is colder than the warm air. Occlusions can still be called cold or warm, however, because what matters is not the actual temperature of the air, but whether air ahead of a front or occlusion is warmer or cooler than the air behind it. In a cold occlusion the air ahead of the front is warmer than the air behind it and in a warm occlusion the air ahead is cooler.

coast. As figure 5 shows, during its 3,000-mile journey across the Atlantic it warms and water starts evaporating into it. It becomes a maritime air mass again, bringing uniform, moist conditions to western Europe and losing a substantial proportion of its water vapor when it crosses the coast and is forced to rise. Even in a country as small as Britain, the annual precipitation on the western side of the country is markedly higher than that on the eastern side and the difference between extreme summer and winter temperatures is less pronounced. These climatic differences are reflected in farming patterns and the landscapes they produce, which makes them immediately visible. Mild, wet conditions favor dairy, beef, and sheep farming. These predominate in the west of the country, with small fields securely bounded by hedges and much of the area growing pasture. Farms in the east, where the climate is drier and summer temperatures more suitable for ripening, grow mainly arable crops, in much larger, more open fields.

A steady progression of air, moving at a constant speed and repeatedly acquiring new characteristics as it crosses continents and oceans, might account for the "average" weather in each region, but it cannot explain certain types of extreme weather. These require an element of conflict and the atmosphere generates plenty.

Not all air masses travel at the same speed. Cold air usually moves faster than warm air. Because of the difference in their densities, masses of air at substantially different temperatures mix very slowly, the warmer tending to form a distinct layer above the cooler. You can demonstrate this for yourself, using water rather than air (see experiment 10 in *A Chronology of Weather*). Advancing cold air undercuts the warmer, slower-moving air ahead of it, lifting it above the surface. Where two air masses meet the boundary between them is called a *front* (see box on page 14) and it is along fronts that extreme weather is most likely to occur.

Nor is the march of the air masses constant. Dense air may become stuck, remaining in the same place for days or weeks. It is then called a *blocking high* and brings dry, settled weather, extremely cold in winter and hot in summer. Despite blocking the path of other air masses, it does not halt their progress. They are diverted around it.

Eddies can develop in the moving air. Sometimes these are 1,000 miles in diameter and last for several days, producing areas of relatively high or low surface pressure called *anticyclones* and *cyclones* (or *depressions*) respectively.

Through all this apparent turmoil, an overall pattern emerges of regions where the surface pressure is usually high and others where it is usually low. "High" and "low" are relative terms, as are "warm" and "cold." Pressure is "high" if it is higher than that of adjacent air,

Figure 6: *Usual distribution of air pressure over North America.*

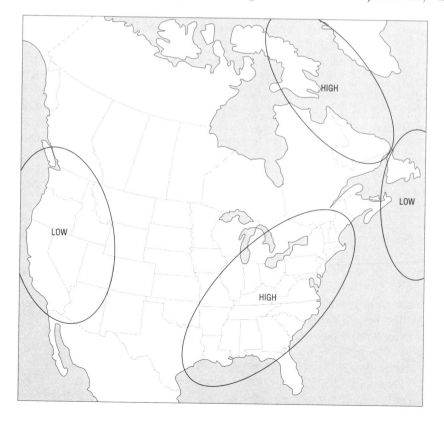

and the temperature can be low in air in the "warm" sector ahead of a "cold" front, provided it is lower still in the "cold" air behind the front. Figure 6 shows the usual distribution of air pressure over North America. Low-pressure areas are centered along the Pacific and Atlantic coasts. High pressure is centered over northeast Canada, where the air is cold, and over the southwest of the United States, where it is warm.

This is the distribution of pressure that results from the eastward movement of air masses. Over the Pacific, maritime air produces the low pressure in the west. As the air mass crosses the continent and becomes increasingly continental, its pressure increases to produce the two high-pressure regions. Maritime air over the Atlantic produces the low-pressure in the east. The pressure distribution is fairly constant, but it results from the ceaseless movement of air.

Ice caps, glaciers, and icebergs

Blizzards consist of snow blown by the wind, and snow is a form of ice. Water freezes whenever the temperature falls below about 32° F. It is necessary to use the word *about* because impurities in the water slightly alter its freezing temperature and so does pressure. Seawater, for example, contains about 35 parts of salt for every thousand parts of water. The salt is mainly sodium chloride (NaCl, or table salt) but a variety of other metal salts are also present. With this concentration of salt, the freezing temperature of water, at average sea level atmospheric pressure, is about 28.5° F. With experiment 14 in *A Chronology of Weather* you can measure this difference in freezing temperature.

The freezing temperature also decreases by 0.014° F for every one-atmosphere (1,000 millibars, or 14.7 pounds per square inch) increase in pressure. This effect is very small, but extremely important. Atmospheric pressure cannot double, but the weight of other substances can easily amount to more than 30 pounds per square inch and melt a layer of ice. When you ice-skate on one foot, for example, the whole weight of your body is carried by the edge of the blade of that skate. If you weigh, say, 110 pounds, your skate exerts a pressure on the ice of about 47 pounds per square inch. Such "pressure melting" explains why some glaciers flow, how ice skaters are able to glide so smoothly over the surface, and why ice is slippery. You can demonstrate the effect very simply (see experiment 15 in *A Chronology of Weather*).

Temperatures fall below freezing in winter in many parts of the world, but in some they seldom rise above it. Thule, on the coast of northern Greenland, has average temperatures above freezing from June to September, but they rise to a maximum of only 46° F and they fall below freezing at night in June and September. In Antarctica temperatures rarely rise above freezing, even in summer, except briefly at the northernmost tip of the Antarctic Peninsula.

In many other parts of the world there are mountains high enough to have temperatures below freezing throughout the year, even in quite low latitudes. In the Himalayan valleys, temperatures in May and June reach about 100° F, but above 15,000 feet they remain below freezing all year around. As they climb, mountaineers move from a tropical to an Arctic climate, passing through temperate regions on the way. There are also permanent glaciers above 14,000 feet in Kenya, on the volcanic peaks of Mt. Kilimanjaro, Mt. Kenya, and Mt. Ruwenzori.

Where summer temperatures remain below freezing, or rise only briefly to slightly above it, snow does not melt. Each time it snows, the fresh snow lies on top of earlier falls and it stays there. Snow accumulates year after year and century after century. In time, the ground is buried deep beneath a thick layer of snow. There is some snow loss. Strong winds blow loose snow up from the surface. The result is a blizzard, and blizzards may blow snow out over the sea or into an area where summers are a little warmer, and the snow will disappear. Snow can also evaporate directly into very dry air. This direct change from solid to gas is called *sublimation.*

Where snow accumulates long enough it turns into ice. Polar and glacier ice do not form in the same way as the ice cubes you make in a freezer. Freezer ice is water that has been frozen, but over the ice sheets it is not water that falls, but snow. The water is already frozen when it reaches the ground as snow. What changes the snow into solid ice is the weight of snow pressing down above it. You can see the start of this process when ordinary winter snow is packed down by people walking or cars driving over it. The snow becomes much more solid than it was when it first fell and you can no longer shovel it the way you shovel fresh snow. You have to chip it away in blocks. It is still snow, however. If the pressure on it had been very much greater the snow would have turned into ice.

The Arctic and Antarctic ice caps and mountain glaciers are made from ice formed in this way, and scientists believe ice has been accumulating in Antarctica for many millions of years. Not surprisingly it has grown very thick over that long period. The thickness varies from place to place, but on average it is about 6,900 feet and it contains a total of more than 11.5 million cubic miles of ice. That is around 90% of all the ice in the world. There is more ice in the Antarctic than in the Arctic because Antarctica is a continent and most of the area within the Arctic Circle is sea. The sea is affected by warm currents flowing north (see page 7) and these prevent

Figure 7: *Boston Glacier,*
the single largest glacier in
the North Cascades, on
September 17, 1960. North
Cascades National Park,
Skagit County,
Washington. (Courtesy of
U.S. Geological Survey)

temperatures falling as low as those in Antarctica. Greenland is the largest land area in the Arctic. There, ice covers more than 708,000 square miles to an average thickness of about 5,000 feet. Between them, the polar ice caps together with mountain glaciers in lower latitudes hold three-quarters of all the fresh water on Earth.

A large expanse of thick ice is called an *ice sheet* or a *glacier.* The two words mean the same thing and, although many people think of a glacier as a river of ice, scientists use them interchangeably. Whichever name you use, if it is thick enough the ice will usually flow.

Most land is not level. Snow may fill the valleys and hide the hills so the surface looks level, but the solid ground still slopes beneath the snow. Once a covering of snow is thick enough, its own weight compresses the lower layers into ice. At the base of the ice the weight may then exert enough pressure to raise the freezing temperature. The increase may be small but just enough to melt the bottom of the ice. When pressure melting happens, the ice is able to move. The bottom layer will flow downhill very slowly, carrying all the overlying ice and snow with it. The entire ice sheet will begin to move. It makes no difference whether the ice covers a broad area or is confined by a high-sided valley; the mechanism is the same. That is why scientists make no distinction between an ice sheet and a glacier.

Glaciers that flow because they melt at the base are known as temperate (or warm). They form far outside the Arctic and Antarctic Circles and move out from large snow and ice fields at higher altitudes, continuing until they reach a level where the temperature is high enough to melt them. Most flow a few inches or a few feet a day, but some can travel as much as 150 feet in a day. Not all the glacier flows at the same speed. Glaciers flow faster at the center than at the sides, where the movement is slowed by friction against the valley walls, and faster in the middle than near the head or foot, and the surface flows more slowly than the ice beneath. It is the movement at the base that carries all the overlying ice with it and this uneven flow causes long, deep cracks, called crevasses, in the brittle upper layers. The surface of a glacier is very uneven and in places it may consist of a jumbled mass of ice blocks called a *sérac*.

Figure 8: *View of Saskatchewan Glacier, a tongue of the Columbia Ice Field, from Parker Ridge, southeast of Mount Athabasca in Alberta, Canada, on August 2, 1954.* (Courtesy of U.S. Geological Survey)

Polar (or cold) glaciers form in high latitudes, where the climate is very much colder and the temperature at the base of the glacier is well below the pressure melting point. The ice will still move, even if there is no melting at its base, when its weight is sufficient to push the middle and upper layers down the slope, dragging the lower layers with them. Because no melting is involved, polar glaciers flow more slowly than temperate glaciers.

When it meets an obstacle, a moving ice sheet will be pushed hard against it by the weight of ice behind that is still flowing downhill. The forward edge will be forced upward against the obstruction. Many mountain glaciers end in an upturned section called a *snout*. Provided it has not entered a region where temperatures are above freezing for several months of the year, the obstacle may check the flow only temporarily. In time, as the pressure is sustained and more snow continues to fall and thicken the sheet, the ice will cross the obstacle and continue on its way.

Eventually the ice sheet arrives at a coast. This does not halt its progress. The ice presses on along the sea bed where the water is shallow until it reaches deeper water, where it floats (see page 70). Ice now extends beyond the coastline and hides it completely. In Antarctica, the ice sheet floats out over the sea to form huge ice shelves. The largest are in the Ross and Weddell seas, the Ross Sea ice shelf being the size of France; big ice shelves are between about 550 feet and more than 1,000 feet thick. There are fewer ice shelves in the Arctic.

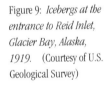

Figure 9: *Icebergs at the entrance to Reid Inlet, Glacier Bay, Alaska, 1919.* (Courtesy of U.S. Geological Survey)

Near the coast, an ice shelf rests securely on the land or the shallow sea bed. Further out, however, where the ice floats, it is not well secured. From time to time a section breaks away from the edge of the shelf as an *iceberg*. In the Antarctic, icebergs are often

shaped like tables, flat-topped, up to about 115 feet high, and often several square miles in area. A few icebergs form in the Arctic in the same way and can drift for years in the Arctic Ocean. They are called *ice islands* and scientific bases have been established on some of them to monitor their movements. Most Arctic icebergs are not like this, however. They are made from ice that has broken away from valley glaciers flowing into the sea from the surrounding lands, rather than ice shelves. This makes them denser than Antarctic icebergs, because they form under greater pressure, and darker in color, because they contain much more soil and rock scoured from the land surface and the sides of their valleys. Few are more than about half a mile long, but they can rise nearly 200 feet above the sea surface and extend more than 800 feet below it. Freed from the main body of ice, they drift with the ocean currents and sometimes enter shipping lanes. In 1912, a collision with one such iceberg sank the liner *Titanic*. For this reason their positions are monitored and reported to ships. As they enter warmer waters they start to melt and break into smaller pieces. An iceberg about the size of a house is called a *bergy bit* and one less than 30 feet long is a *growler*.

Figure 10 shows how far icebergs can travel in the North Atlantic and around Antarctica before they melt completely. The maps also show the area within which the sea itself freezes, the edge of the sea ice advancing in winter and retreating in summer, but with a considerable area that remains frozen permanently. Winds and waves constantly break up sea ice while it is forming. They carry it this way and that, piling it into various shapes. It is called *pack ice* when it covers a large area. Sailors know when they are approaching pack ice. They see what looks like a white light above the horizon, caused by light reflected from the ice.

When sea water freezes, the salt is left behind and crystals of freshwater ice form (in experiment 14, *A Chronology of Weather*, you are invited to taste ice made by freezing salt water to check this for yourself). Later, as the crystals start joining together as an oily-looking coating of slush, called *frazil ice*, pockets of salt water are trapped between crystals. At first the ice contains no salt, but the water adjacent to the ice is more salty than water further away because it contains the "squeezed-out" salt. This added salt makes the water denser and lowers its freezing temperature. It is also at the temperature at which water reaches its maximum density (see page 74). This dense water sinks to the ocean floor and flows south as a slow-moving current called the North Atlantic Deep Water (NADW), which travels all the way to Antarctica. Its place at the surface is taken by warmer water flowing north. This is how the formation of sea ice in the North Atlantic drives the system of ocean currents.

Sea ice affects the climate in another way. Farmers and gardeners know that a cover of snow protects the plants beneath it by insulating them. Snow is a poor conductor of heat, so once it has

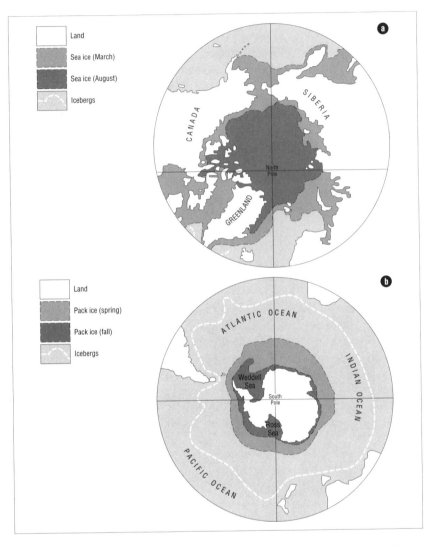

Figure 10a: *Sea ice and icebergs in the Arctic.*
Figure 10b: *Pack ice and icebergs in the Antarctic.*

fallen it reduces greatly any further cooling of the covered surface. Snow also falls on frozen sea, and because the temperature of the sea ice is already below freezing, it settles. In time it can form a thick layer. This reduces the rate at which the water cools beneath the ice.

The NADW has driven the Gulf Stream system of currents throughout our recorded history. Quite naturally, we think of it as permanent and reliable. Scientists now believe this long period of stability is unusual and that in the past the pattern of ocean currents changed often. When much of northern North America lay beneath the thick Laurentide ice sheet, for example, from time to time vast numbers of icebergs broke away and drifted out to sea. That this happened was discovered some years ago by Hartmut Heinrich, and these iceberg releases are called *Heinrich events.* Icebergs are made from fresh water and when the Laurentide icebergs melted they covered a large part of the ocean with a surface layer of fresh water, floating on top of the denser salt water. This froze at a higher temperature than salt water, chilled the air crossing it, and brought cold weather to the northern hemisphere generally. Europe was especially affected, because the edge of the sea ice shifted, interrupting the formation of NADW. That caused the North Atlantic Drift to cease to flow. The whole of the Gulf Stream turned south in the latitude of Spain, depriving northwestern Europe of the warm water which now bathes its shores.

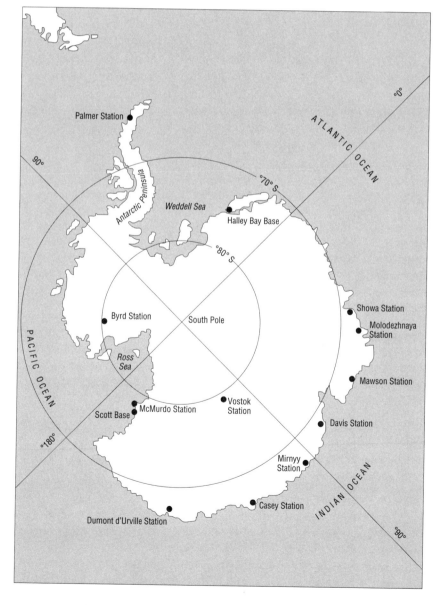

Figure 11: *Antarctica.*

Reading past weather from ice sheets

Antarctica is a harsh, unforgiving place. Apart from tourists who stay a day or two, only scientists spend long periods there and, as figure 11 shows, most of the research stations are near the coast, within easy reach of the ships that supply them. There are about 40 permanently manned and up to 100 temporary research stations on the continent, accommodating rather more than 4,000 scientists during the summer and about 1,000 during the winter. The Amundsen-Scott Station is at the South Pole itself, but the only other permanent inland station is Vostok, the Russian station at about 78° S. Opened in 1957, it stayed open all year round until 1994, when it had to close for the winter because tractor trains were unable to deliver fuel to it from the coast and its staff was compelled to overwinter at the coastal Mirnyy station. It was Vostok scientists who reported the lowest temperature ever recorded on Earth. On August 24, 1960 their thermometers read -126.9° F.

Vostok is located in a place where the ice sheet is very thick, and the Russian and French scientists who work there use the ice sheet itself to study past climates. Two other projects do similar work in the northern hemisphere, at a place called Summit, in central Greenland. The United States operates the Greenland Ice Sheet Project 2 (GISP 2) and about 19 miles away European scientists operate the Greenland Ice Core Project (GRIP). All these research projects involve drilling vertically deep into the ice and removing cores for examination. In 1993, both the Greenland projects reached bedrock beneath the ice sheet at a depth of around 10,000 feet. The cores have revealed a great deal about the world climate back to 150,000 years ago.

With many tree species (but not all) you can tell the age of a tree by counting the annual growth rings. Each spring and early summer the tree produces new cells. These are large, with thin walls and pale in color. In late summer it produces smaller cells, with thicker walls, which are dark in color. By counting the rings it is possible not only to calculate the age of the tree, but also the growing conditions each year, because trees grow faster, producing wider rings, in good weather than in bad weather. It is not necessary to fell the tree in order to examine its rings. A drill with a hollow cylindrical cutter can take a thin core of wood which serves just as well. Ice cores are very much like this, only thicker, and they can be dated in the same way, because each year's accumulation of snow is compressed into a layer that can be seen as a band. This allows scientists to mark each core with a scale of years before they take samples for analysis. These samples include the ice itself, tiny

Figure 12: *In central Greenland, members of the Greenland Ice Sheet Project II collect an ice core sample, 4 inches in diameter, from the barrel of one of their smaller drills.* (Courtesy of Fr. Richard B. Alley, Pennsylvania State University)

air bubbles trapped in the ice, and solid particles that fell onto the ice and were then buried.

Ice is made from water, and every water molecule comprises one atom of hydrogen and two of oxygen, but not all oxygen atoms are identical. There are three common forms (*isotopes*) of oxygen, written as ^{16}O, ^{17}O, and ^{18}O. Chemically the atoms are exactly the same, but the higher the isotope number, the heavier the atom. When scientists analyze ice cores, they are interested only in ^{16}O and ^{18}O. In the atmosphere today there is about one atom of ^{18}O to every 500 atoms of ^{16}O, but in water and ice these proportions may be different. Water molecules containing ^{16}O (written as $H_2^{16}O$) are lighter than $H_2^{18}O$ molecules and they evaporate at a slightly lower temperature. In warm weather, therefore, the atmosphere contains a higher proportion of ^{16}O and, as this water falls in precipitation, so does rain and, in polar regions, snow. The lower the proportion of ^{18}O compared with ^{16}O in the ice, the colder the air was when the original snow fell.

When snow is compacted into ice, countless tiny bubbles of air are trapped in it. These are also analyzed. Scientists believe the proportion of ^{18}O in air depends on the proportion in sea water and that depends, in turn, on how much water ($H_2^{16}O$) has evaporated and then accumulated in the polar ice sheets. So by examining the oxygen trapped in air bubbles they can calculate the size of the ice sheets at the time the snow fell. Ice sheets grow by accumulating water evaporated from the sea. This alters the sea level because when water is taken from the sea its level falls, so the oxygen in ice cores also provides information about past sea levels. If the present Antarctic ice sheet were to melt, for example, seas throughout the world would rise, probably by up to 200 feet, and then, over thousands of years, the ocean floors would sink under the additional weight of water, lowering sea level by about 65 feet, and Antarctica itself would rise because the weight of the ice had been removed. Sea levels are affected by factors other than the size of the ice sheets, but none produces effects so quickly.

Even with global warming, no one supposes this will happen in the foreseeable future. The Antarctic ice sheet is very stable. Some of the ice shelves have grown much smaller, but this has no effect on sea level because shelf ice is already in the sea and does not add any more water to it if the ice melts.

Air bubbles have still more to tell. As well as oxygen and nitrogen, the principal constituents of our atmosphere, they contain carbon dioxide and methane. These are so-called "greenhouse gases," which absorb longwave radiation and warm the atmosphere (see page 116). If the bubbles contain more or less of them than the air does today, it suggests that when they became trapped between snow crystals the air was warmer or cooler than it is now. This is only part of their story, however. Although scientists are confident that if we add more of these gases to the air the climate will grow warmer, it does not follow that in the distant past warming and cooling were caused by changes in the concentration of them. The changes may have been a response to climate change, rather than its cause.

Apart from certain bacteria, all living things obtain the energy they need by oxidizing carbon, a chemical reaction that releases energy and produces carbon dioxide that is returned to the air. The process is *respiration* (not to be confused with breathing, which is the means we use to take oxygen into and remove carbon dioxide from our bodies). Plants obtain carbon by the process of photosynthesis and animals by consuming the carbon in plants or in other animals.

Ordinarily, the amount of carbon dioxide removed from the air by photosynthesis is equal to the amount returned to the air by respiration, so the atmospheric concentration of carbon dioxide remains constant. If living conditions suddenly improve, however, plants will grow more vigorously and use more carbon dioxide. For a time, the atmospheric concentration will fall. The balance will be restored when animals increase in number because more food is available and respiration catches up with photosynthesis. In deteriorating conditions plants will grow less well and there will be less food for animals. As the total quality of living material (called the *biomass*) becomes smaller, respiration by organisms that decompose formerly living matter will overtake photosynthesis and surplus carbon dioxide will accumulate in the atmosphere. The carbon dioxide content of the air is difficult to interpret, but it can give clues to climates of the past.

Methane is easier to understand. It is released by certain groups of bacteria, some of which live in the digestive system of animals but most of which live below the surface in waterlogged mud. Oxygen poisons them if it occurs free, as a gas, so they inhabit only airless places. They thrive best in warm conditions, so the warmer the climate the more active they will be and, therefore, the more methane they will release. The concentration of methane scientists find in air bubbles trapped in ice cores is never high (the present atmosphere contains about 1.7 parts of methane for every million parts of air by volume). Today, human activities add to the amount in the air, but changes in the concentration in air in ice cores reflect changes in the climate when the air was trapped.

It is not only air that ice sheets collect. They also collect dust. This, too, contains clues to past climates.

Air always contains dust, but the amount varies. You can find out for yourself the extent to which different kinds of weather produce different amounts of airborne dust (see experiment 16 in *A Chronology of Weather*). Rain and snow wash dust particles from the air. That is why the air often feels much fresher after a shower. Individual dust particles rarely remain airborne for more than a few days before being washed to the ground, but they can stay aloft much longer in dry weather.

When the Sun is low in the sky, around dawn and sunset, its light has to pass through a greater thickness of air than when it is higher. If there are enough dust particles in the air they will scatter the shorter blue, green, and yellow wavelengths of light so only red light passes and the sky looks red in the direction of the Sun. The dust indicates dusty air, which is therefore dry, and dry air means fine weather. In middle latitudes, weather systems usually travel from west to east, so if you see a red sky at sunset, in the west, the dry air that causes it will reach you in a few hours and the following day will be fine (unless the system is moving so fast that the fine weather passes you during the night). A red sky at dawn, on the other hand, means the dry air is to the east and has already passed, so there is no guarantee of a fine day to follow. This, of course, is the origin of the old saying: "Red sky at night, shepherd's delight / Red sky in the morning, shepherd's warning." It is one piece of weather lore that is fairly reliable.

Eventually, all the dust falls to the ground. Rain and snow simply bring it down faster, often before it has had time to travel very far. Once an ice sheet covers land, dust can no longer be blown up from the surface, so dust in the air over an ice sheet has probably traveled a long way. For that to have happened the air must have been dry over a large part of the planet. Dust falling on an ice sheet sticks to the ice crystals and in time is buried beneath later falls of snow. In this way it becomes incorporated in the ice and can be detected in ice cores. If these show that the amount of dust increased during a particular period, it strongly suggests the global climate during that period was relatively dry.

Over the world as a whole, dry weather means cold weather. When temperatures are low, less water evaporates, so there is less cloud and, therefore, less rain and snow. If the weather remains cold for a long time, the ice sheets and glaciers will expand. They take water from the sea, causing the sea level to fall, and the fall in sea level exposes more dry land. Overall, more land is exposed than is covered by the ice sheets themselves, and the combined effect of an increased land area and generally dry climates is to allow more dust to be blown into the air.

The dust trapped in ancient ice thus provides another clue to past weather, but the type of dust also provides valuable clues. Volcanic eruptions inject vast quantities of dust into the air and volcanic dust can be identified. This knowledge is valuable, because volcanic eruptions sometimes affect the climate. Much of the volcanic dust is washed to the ground in a matter of days, like any other dust, but a really violent eruption can throw minute particles into the stratosphere, where they remain for months or even years. They consist mainly of sulfur dioxide that reacts to form microscopically small droplets of sulfuric acid. These particles reflect incoming sunlight, cooling the surface beneath them, and stratospheric air currents can spread this volcanic blanket right around the world, producing a marked cooling in the climate. When Mt. Pinatubo, in the Philippines, erupted in June 1991, within three weeks a belt of sulfuric acid particles covered 40% of the world and reduced surface temperatures for several years, but some past eruptions have had a much greater effect. The eruption of Mt. Tambora, in what is now Indonesia, threw about 35 cubic miles of dust and fragments into the air. That eruption was in 1815, and because of the particles it threw into the stratosphere, 1816 became known as the year with no summer. Mt. Krakatau, which erupted in 1883, ejected about five cubic miles of material and caused magnificent red sunsets the following year, as well as a slight fall in temperature.

Ice cores record the evidence of past volcanic activity and this can be related to changes in climate. Usually these are small, but if the climate was already starting to cool, a violent eruption might accelerate the process.

Scientists who study very ancient climates are called *paleo-climatologists*. The weather leaves many clues. Lakebed and seabed sediments store information much like that contained in ice sheets, but in most cases they have accumulated over a shorter period and their record is not so long. Pollen grains, which are covered in a coat so tough they survive in the soil almost indefinitely, can be identified as coming from particular kinds of plants, and most plants grow only in certain climates. Many small animals survive only within a narrow temperature and humidity range. Beetles are especially useful in this respect and so are some marine animals. Corals, for example, build reefs only in clear water, about 30–200 feet deep, at a temperature between 68° F and 82° F. Some fossil reefs are much thicker than 200 feet, suggesting they continued to grow upward as the sea level slowly rose.

Corals, the wing cases (elytra) of beetles, and pollen grains are valuable indicators of past climates. Much can also be read from the landscape itself. Valleys and lakes made by glaciers are not difficult to recognize. Yet none of these provides the continuous record over more than 100,000 years that can be read from ice cores.

The more we know about past climates the better we will be able to calculate ways in which the climates of the world may change in years to come. We will learn how resistant to change climates are and what is most likely to trigger changes. Some change is inevitable because the climate is changing constantly. How it changes will determine whether severe winter storms and blizzards come to afflict wider areas in the future, or whether they retreat until they survive only in history books.

Polar deserts, where blizzards are common

Blizzards happen suddenly in polar regions. Most of the time the sky is clear blue and the light reflected by the snow is dazzling, so travelers wear dark glasses to protect their eyes. The air is almost still. Then, without warning, the wind starts to blow, quickly picking up to 30 MPH or more, with frequent gusts at more than twice that speed. Loose snow is blown up from the surface into a great, whirling cloud. Everything is white, the sky merging with the land so it is impossible to tell where one ends and the other begins. Visibility is reduced to a few yards and for the traveler there is no alternative but to stop. Landmarks have vanished, all directions look the same, and although the compass might indicate the direction in which to proceed it cannot reveal obstacles, such as deep crevasses, that would necessitate detours. In winter, of course, blizzards are even more bewildering, because they happen in twilight or total darkness. The only consolation they bring is that Antarctic winter blizzards bring a rapid rise in temperature of up to 32° F, but very few people venture far from shelter in winter. In summer, blizzards are cold. The temperature falls.

Once a blizzard starts there is no telling how long it may last. Some fade after a few hours, others continue for days. At the end of their ill-fated march to the South Pole in 1912, a blizzard that lasted nine days confined the three survivors of the Scott expedition to their tent, where their frozen bodies were found some months later. In the Antarctic winter of 1989 a party set out to cross the continent. They encountered strong winds, sometimes reaching 90 MPH, for almost the whole of their journey and temperatures fell to -49° F. One storm lasted 60 days and they endured a blizzard that continued for 17 days. A member of the team became lost in a blizzard one evening only a few yards from the camp and had to dig a trench in which he lay while the snow covered him. His colleagues rescued him, cold but unharmed, the following morning.

Some places have more blizzards than others, and generally there are more polar blizzards in winter than in summer. On its return from the Pole, the Scott expedition suffered frequent and fierce blizzards, but the party led by Roald Amundsen, traveling at much the same time but further to the east, enjoyed good weather with only light winds. Adélie Land, the region of Antarctica nearest Tasmania, has been called the home of the blizzard and at Byrd Station (see the map on page 25) the winds are strong enough to produce blizzards for about 65% of the time and for nearly one-third of the time these reduce visibility to zero.

Snow covers the ground and most of the sea throughout the year inside the Arctic and Antarctic Circles, so the raw material for blizzards is always present. As figure 13a shows, comparatively little land lies north of the Arctic Circle. Whenever the sea beneath the pack ice cools below 29° F, heat transferred from the ice and open water warms it again, so the sea remains at about 29° F, even during the long winter night. At the North Pole itself, the night lasts 176 days and at Spitzbergen it lasts 150 days. Above the ice, temperatures range from about -140° F in winter to 4° F in summer.

Northern Canada and Greenland have Arctic climates. As figure 13b shows, to the south of this permanently frozen region, a broad belt crossing Canada east of the Rockies has a subarctic climate, where temperatures rise above freezing in summer, supporting tundra vegetation comprising mainly lichens, herbs, and scattered dwarf shrubs and trees. It is a region of calm weather and storms are uncommon. Weather systems moving eastward, which might bring stormy conditions, tend to be checked by the mountains.

On average, the Arctic is about 30° F warmer than Antarctica, where average annual temperatures range from -2° F to -70° F and

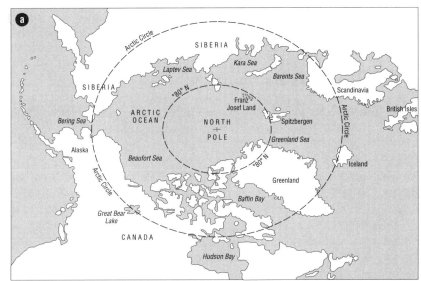

Figure 13a: *The Arctic.*
Figure 13b: *North American Arctic.*

summer lasts for only two months while the winter lasts for six. This difference is due partly to the influence of the sea in the Arctic, combined with the high elevation of much of Antarctica. The two sides of the continent are divided by the Transantarctic Mountain Range and the South Pole is 10,000 feet above sea level. It is also due to the fact that in winter the South Pole is three million miles farther from the Sun than the North Pole is during its winter, so in their respective winters Antarctica receives about 7% less solar radiation than the Arctic. Over the year, the Antarctic radiates more heat into space than it receives from the Sun, but is warmed by incoming air and sea from higher latitudes.

Where the snow, compacted into ice, lies more than a mile thick it is reasonable to suppose snow must fall frequently and heavily. It does not, and despite the ice sheets, not everywhere is covered by snow. In the northern tundra the winter snow is not deep, except where it has drifted, and the ground is exposed over large areas. Even in Antarctica there are dry valleys, with no snow, and where snowfalls are frequent they are usually light. Both the polar regions are dry deserts. Their snow coverings accumulate because when snow does fall the temperature never rises sufficiently to melt it.

Snow is much bulkier than rain because of the pockets of air held between its grains, and some kinds of snow are bulkier than others. When snow is expected, forecasters often estimate the amount people are likely to receive, giving a figure in inches. This represents a depth of snow and the information is helpful, but if the amount of precipitation in two places is to be compared it is best to convert snowfall to its rainfall equivalent. Then water is being compared with water and there can be no confusion. After the snow has fallen, an open cylinder is pressed vertically through the snow to remove a core, one end of the cylinder is sealed, the snow is melted, and the depth of water measured. As a rule of thumb, 10 inches of snow is equivalent to one inch of rain.

Deserts form wherever the amount of rain or snow that falls is less than the amount which can evaporate from the surface during the same period. Obviously, this depends on the air temperature, but deserts occur anywhere in the world if the annual precipitation is less than 10 inches. For comparison, the average annual precipitation in New York is 43 inches and in Dublin, on the other side of the ocean, it is 29.7 inches. Figure 14 shows these beside the average annual rainfall at Touggourt, in one of the driest parts of the Sahara. Touggourt has an average of 2.9 inches of rain a year. Thule, however, on the northwest coast of Greenland, receives only 2.5 inches of precipitation a year and the South Pole 2.8 inches (in both cases as rainfall equivalent). Of the snow falling at the South Pole, 1.2 inches are lost by sublimation (changing directly from ice to vapor) and being blown away by the wind (this process is called *ablation*). Both are drier than the Sahara and in inland Antarctica

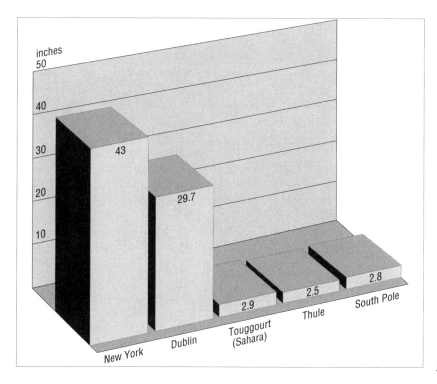

inches
50
40
30
20
10

43

29.7

2.9

2.5

2.8

New York

Dublin

Touggourt
(Sahara)

Thule

South Pole

Figure 14: *Average annual precipitation.*

the relative humidity is often only 1%. (Relative humidity is the amount of water vapor present in the air as a percentage of the amount needed to saturate the air at that temperature; in New York relative humidity is usually around 55 to 60%).

Warm air can hold more water vapor than cold air, so the colder the air the drier it will be. As its temperature falls, more of its water vapor will condense. Air at 68° F can hold 12 times more water vapor than air at 32° F and at -40° F air can hold almost no water vapor at all. Polar air is chilled until it is extremely dry, and that is why the polar regions are deserts.

Blizzards are mainly caused by loose snow blown into the air by the wind. In Greenland, areas of low atmospheric pressure (depressions) passing near the coast cause winds that draw very cold air from the high ground inland, down the glaciated valleys. Depressions also develop in the oceans bordering Antarctica and cause gales around those coasts. Polar depressions are circular in shape, like tropical cyclones, and less than about 300 miles across. They produce violent storms with steady winds of 45 MPH or so, gusting to 70 MPH, and are sometimes called *extratropical hurricanes*.

Other winds, capable of reaching gale force, are caused by the very low polar temperatures. Ice sheets are not simply vast areas of flat ice. Because the ice flows outward from the center (see page 20), ice sheets are domed. Their sides may not slope very steeply, although in places they do, but a shallow gradient is enough to start air moving. Over the center of the dome temperatures are at their lowest. Being so cold, the lower layer of air is dense and the surface pressure high. The air cannot rise because it is cooled from below by its contact with the ice, so the air above it is warmer. This is a *temperature inversion*, a layer of air that is warmer than the air below it. Temperature inversions trap the lower air, which cannot rise because it is denser than the layer of air overlying it. Over the polar ice domes, the temperature in the inversion is often about 45° F, which is much warmer than the air near the surface, so the inversion is strong. Instead of rising, the very cold air flows downhill. A wind comprising cold, dense air flowing down a slope is called *katabatic* and its speed depends on the difference between the air pressure at the top and bottom of the slope. The wind is strongest when pressure at the top of the dome is higher than that lower down, but the dense air is also moving under gravity, like water flowing down a hillside. This means the wind can continue blowing even when pressure is higher at a low level than it is higher up, although then the wind is not so strong. Over much of Antarctica the prevailing winds are katabatic and blow from the south, for much of the time with great force. They produce waves in the snow, like sand dunes, some more than 6 feet high. It is these winds that cause blizzards, especially when they are funneled through high-sided valleys, which accelerates them.

Louis Agassiz and the Great Ice Age

Each year the seasons follow one another. Spring may arrive a little early or late, summer may be warmer or cooler than it was last year, winter may bring more or less snow than usual, but the progression is orderly and the variation small. Over the course of a human lifetime, the climate remains fairly constant. When you look at the world around you and talk to elderly people about their childhood memories, there seems no reason to suppose that the weather ever really changes. Until quite recently, that is the way everyone thought things were: The kind of weather we experience now would be no different from the weather the Romans knew, or people who lived in Old Testament times, or the weather that had existed for countless thousands of years.

In Europe, however, there was a puzzle to do not with the weather as such, but with certain rocks. A century ago, geologists were busily classifying rocks and reconstructing landscapes of the past, but these particular rocks did not fit. They were boulders and piles of gravel lying at the surface or buried just beneath it. Boulders are common enough, but usually they are similar to the solid rock nearby and from which they have clearly been broken. These rocks, however, were nothing like the neighboring rocks, but closely resembled rock formations hundreds of miles away. Geologists call them *erratics* and the puzzle was how they came to be where they were found. For a long time it was assumed they had been washed down from the uplands by the Biblical flood.

There was one clue, but it did not make much sense either. There is often a jumble of rocks called a *moraine* at the lower end of a glacier, and it includes rocks that apparently have been transported from far away. Perhaps the erratics had been transported in the same way. The difficulty was that no one knew how glacial moraines occurred. If you look at a glacier, or stand on one, what you see is a solid mass of ice with a very rough, broken surface. The ice is not moving. At least, you cannot see it move, although now and then you may hear strange creaking noises from it. Nevertheless, by early in the last century some scientists were speculating that glaciers do, in fact, move, that moraines are made from material the moving glacier has scoured from its bed and sides and then pushed ahead of itself, and that the erratics had been deposited by glaciers that had since disappeared. Only no one had been able to prove even that glaciers move.

That proof came around 1840, not from a geologist but from a zoologist. Louis Agassiz (1807–73), the professor of natural history at the University of Neuchâtel, was already a distinguished ichthyologist (a scientist who studies fishes) and a leading authority on fossil fishes. He was Swiss (see *A Chronology of Weather* for more details of his life) and familiar with glaciers when, in 1836 and 1837, he spent his vacations studying them with friends. They built a hut on the Aar glacier to use as a base and called it the Hôtel des Neuchâtelois.

Boulders and smaller rock fragments lay along the sides of the glacier, looking for all the world as though they had been torn away by the ice. When Agassiz and his friends examined them closely they found some of them marked with parallel grooves. These could have been made by stones partially embedded in the ice and dragged over softer rock.

Between vacations, Agassiz wrote up the notes he had made and each year he returned. In 1839 he came across another hut. Agassiz found it almost a mile away from the place where it was known to have been erected in 1827. It must have been carried by the glacier. To check this, in 1840 he drove a line of stakes directly across the glacier, from one side to the other, fixing them in the ice as firmly as he could. A year later, when he returned, the line was no longer straight. It now made a U shape and the whole line had moved from its original position. Friction between the rocks and ice at the sides of the glacier slowed its movement there, but the middle of the glacier moved faster.

He had shown conclusively that glaciers flow. This being so, the moraines that line the sides of glaciers and pile up at their ends (*terminal moraines*) were explained. Glaciers scour away rock, carry it with them, and deposit some of it at their ends, at a level where the air temperature is high enough to melt the ice. The erratic boulders and gravel deposits that had proved so puzzling looked just like those deposited by glaciers. If that is how they had reached their present positions, the glaciers responsible had since disappeared. Glaciers retreat when temperatures rise because the point at which the ice melts advances to higher levels. Conversely, when temperatures fall, glaciers advance. Assuming they really were glacial in origin, the position of the erratics marked the lower boundaries of something more significant than a few individual glaciers. Agassiz concluded first that at one time, not very far in the geological past, the whole of Switzerland had lain beneath a single ice sheet. He extended his study of glacial deposits, visiting Scotland in 1840, and came to realize that much of Europe had once been covered by an ice sheet resembling that which still covered Greenland.

He published his discoveries in 1840, in a book called *Études sur les glaciers*. His idea was not entirely original. A German professor

Figure 15: *Maximum extent of the ice sheet in North America.*

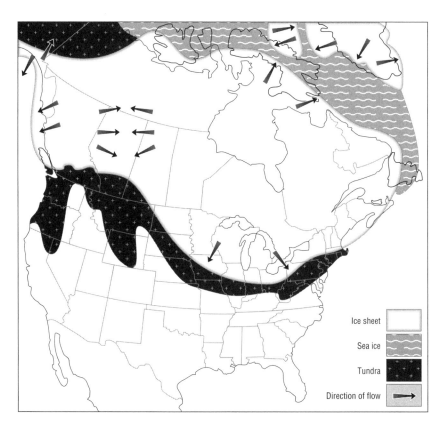

of forestry, A. Bernhardi, had proposed it in 1832, and shortly after Agassiz published his book, a Swiss superintendent of mines, Jean de Charpentier (1786–1855), published his own version of the same theory. It was Agassiz who produced the hard evidence and convincing argument, however, and over the next 30 years his idea of a "Great Ice Age" gradually came to be accepted by scientists.

In 1846, King Friedrich Wilhelm IV of Prussia paid for Agassiz to deliver a series of lectures in the United States, mainly about fossil fish, the subject Agassiz had studied for so long. The lectures proved very popular. He extended his visit, then decided to remain permanently, eventually becoming an American citizen. Over the years that followed, he traced the boundaries of the ice sheet that once covered a large part of North America, establishing that his Great Ice Age had affected the whole of the northern hemisphere. Figure 15 shows the extent of the North American ice sheet and sea ice. In 1848 he was appointed professor of zoology at Harvard and in 1859 achieved one of his ambitions with the founding at Harvard of what is now called the Agassiz Museum of Comparative Zoology.

New ideas are often controversial. This one was no exception, which is why it came to be accepted only gradually. When Agassiz proposed it, a fierce argument among scientists had been raging for years, between *catastrophists* and *uniformitarians.* Catastrophists held that the history of the Earth is dominated by sudden, violent events. Uniformitarians, on the other hand, believed that change is gradual and continuous, so that processes we can observe today have operated throughout history and can explain fully the formation of the world we see around us. Agassiz was a catastrophist (who suggested the Great Ice Age had destroyed all life on Earth) and his idea contradicted the uniformitarian view that the Earth had been very hot when it first formed and that it had been cooling steadily ever since.

Agassiz went much too far, of course. Ice ages cause some extinctions, but surprisingly few. They certainly do not wipe out all life. He was also wrong on another point. His Great Ice Age was not unique. It occurred during what is now called the Pleistocene Epoch, which began about 2 million years ago and ended about 10,000 years ago, but it was one of several ice ages, or episodes of glacial advance. North America and Europe experienced five ice ages during the Pleistocene (sometimes subdivided to make more). They differed in extent and severity and were separated by warmer periods called *interglacials.* In some interglacials climates were warmer than those of today. About 100,000 years ago, for example, during the Ipswichian Interglacial, rhinoceros, hippopotamus, and elephants lived where London is today and the average temperature was about 4.5° F warmer than it is now. Even the ice ages were not unrelieved periods of bitter cold. They were interrupted by *inter-*

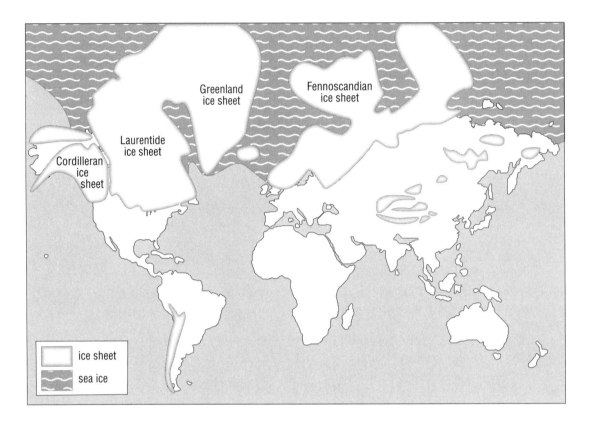

Figure 16: *Earth during the*
Great Ice Age.

stades, episodes of warmer conditions that were shorter and cooler than interglacials.

Scientists believe we are now living in an interglacial, called the Flandrian, and that one day it will end and the ice will return. It began about 10,000 years ago, as the ice sheets retreated at the end of the final ice age of the Pleistocene, known in North America as the Wisconsinian and in Britain as the Devensian (and elsewhere in northern Europe as the Weichselian). This also marked the end of the Pleistocene Epoch. We are now living in the Holocene (or Recent) Epoch.

At their greatest extent, the Pleistocene ice ages buried a substantial part of the world beneath ice. Figure 16 shows the approximate size of the ice sheets, and the names of the biggest. Siberia was not covered by a continuous sheet, but this was due to its extremely dry climate, not warm temperatures. Between the continental ice sheets, the sea was covered in ice shelves and pack ice, so it would have been impossible to tell where continents ended and the sea began. There is less land at high latitudes in the southern hemisphere than in the northern, so the effects were smaller there, but an ice sheet did cover the western side of South America. As the map shows, the world did not look quite as it does today. Sea levels had fallen everywhere and shallow seas became dry land.

Australia was joined to parts of what are now Indonesia, and Alaska was joined to Asia across the Bering Strait.

Ice ages also occurred in earlier times, although the evidence for them is much sparser than for those of the Pleistocene. The ice sheets advanced at least twice between 950 and 615 million years ago. Glaciers left traces in North Africa around 440 million years ago, but no one knows how large an area they covered. There is reason to suppose an ice age occurred about 2.3 billion years ago, affecting what are now North America, South Africa, and Australia.

No one really knows what causes ice ages to begin and end, but there is strong evidence in favor of an idea proposed in 1930 by a Serbian climatologist, Milutin Milankovich. He spent 30 years studying cyclical variations in the rotation of the Earth and its orbit about the Sun. These are very regular, so he could relate them to dates over the past 650,000 years when the cycles were at particular stages. When he did so, he found the cycles corresponded precisely with the known ice ages.

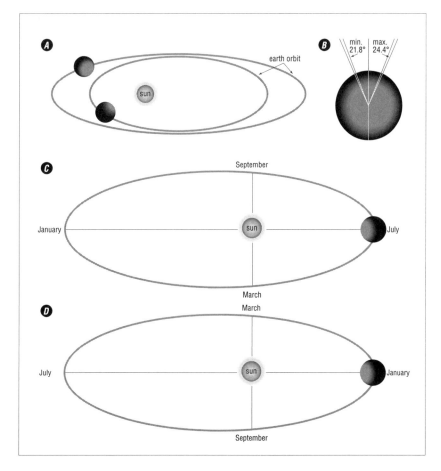

Figure 17: *The Milankovich cycles.*

There are three cycles, shown in figure 17. The first concerns the orbital path Earth follows. Planetary orbits are elliptical in shape, not circular, and the Sun is at one of the two foci of the ellipse. This means the distance between Earth and the Sun varies through the year and, therefore, so does the amount of solar radiation we receive. At present, there is 6% difference between the maximum and minimum. Over a cycle of 100,000 years, the shape of the orbital path changes. The ellipse becomes more elongated, so Earth moves further from the Sun. At the extreme of this cycle, the difference between maximum and minimum radiation is 30%.

The axis of the Earth's rotation is not vertical in relation to solar radiation. Earth is tilted, at present by about 23.5°. Over a 40,000-year cycle, the angle changes, from a minimum of 21.8° to a maximum of 24.4°. This alters the amount of radiation received in high latitudes and, therefore, the extent of the polar ice sheets and sea ice.

The axis also wobbles, describing a small circle, like a toy gyroscope. This is called *precession* and over a cycle of 21,000 years it alters the time of year of the equinoxes, when the axis is perpendicular to the solar radiation. It also alters the time of year when the Earth is closest to the Sun (*perihelion*). At present perihelion is in January, but 10,500 years ago it was in July. This affects the warmth of summers and winters.

By itself, each of these cycles has a very small effect on the amount of radiation the Earth receives, but every so often they coincide. When this happens, the Earth receives markedly more or less radiation. The times when the cycles produced minimum radiation coincide with the onset of ice ages, those when radiation reached a maximum with interglacials.

Much more recently than the end of the Pleistocene, in about 1550, average temperatures fell about 2° F throughout the northern hemisphere and they did not start rising again until 1860. This period is called the Little Ice Age. It brought very severe winters, and glaciers everywhere advanced. Year after year the winter snow failed to melt in southwest Greenland, and everyone living in a Norse colony there died because the pack ice cut them off from the rest of the world. Some scientists suspect that the climatic warming over the last century may be a continuing recovery from the Little Ice Age.

This, too, may have been triggered by the Sun. In 1893, Edward Walter Maunder (1851–1928) discovered that the total number of sunspots reported between 1645 and 1715 was smaller than the number seen nowadays in an average year, and that there was a period of 32 years during which not a single sunspot was recorded. Maunder was then superintendent of the solar division at the Royal Greenwich Observatory in London and had been checking old records. For centuries astronomers have been interested in sunspots, dark patches that appear on the visible surface of the Sun, and have noted their appearance. Maunder wrote several papers on the subject, suggesting that such changes in the Sun might produce effects on Earth. The period he identified became known as the Maunder Minimum, but no one took very much notice until the 1970s, when the matter was taken up by the American solar astronomer John A. Eddy. Sunspot activity affects the rate at which radioactive carbon-14 (^{14}C) is formed in the upper atmosphere, so past sunspot activity can be calculated by analyzing ^{14}C in the growth rings of trees. The ^{14}C record is reliable for the last 5,000 years and Eddy used it to reveal several earlier Maunder Minima. Then he noted that the 1645 to 1715 Maunder Minimum coincides fairly closely with the coldest part of the Little Ice Age. The earlier ones also match glacial advances and, during recorded history, periods of very cold weather. Solar maxima, when sunspot activity was high, coincide with warm periods.

Between them, Milankovich and Maunder have made a convincing link between changes in the amount of radiation we receive from the Sun and the climates of Earth. It is the returning warmth of the Sun that melts the winter snow and heralds summer, but we know now that its output varies and that the orbit and rotation of the Earth alter the amount of radiation we receive. From time to time in the past the winter snow has failed to melt and blizzards have continued through what should have been summer. It has happened before and scientists are confident that one day it will happen again.

Snowblitz

Ice ages can end very quickly. When the temperature starts rising and the ice begins to melt, the process accelerates. Meltwaters flow as rivers. These carry away fine particles and where the river meets the sea, or slows as it crosses level ground, the particles settle and accumulate as sediment. By examining the sediment, scientists can tell how rapidly it was deposited and, from that, how long it took for the ice age to give way to temperate conditions. The entire transition was often completed in a matter of decades, perhaps in as little as 20 years.

Times of very rapid change are not always good times to be around. Change is disruptive, even when the eventual outcome is a good one, and events can get out of control. During the last ice age, a tongue of the ice sheet extended south from British Columbia and blocked the Clark Fork River, near the border between Washington and Idaho. Behind the ice, the river formed a huge lake about

3,000 square miles in surface area and in places 2,000 feet deep. Then, as the ice age approached its end around 15,000 years ago, suddenly the dam broke. All of the water in the lake, all 500 cubic miles of it, emptied within 48 hours. A wave rushed across the lower land at more than 50 MPH, carrying all before it. The glacial lake no longer exists, but to this day, 15,000 years later, the land has not recovered from the onslaught. It forms the Channelled Scabland, 13,000 square miles of a landscape so harsh space scientists study it to help them plan for the next unmanned landing on Mars.

Ice ages may end abruptly, but most scientists believe they start gradually. If one were to commence now it might be many years before we were even aware of it. On the other hand, there is a possibility that it might begin just as rapidly as ice ages can end and that within a century or two what are now the temperate regions north of latitude 50° might be covered in permanent snow, turning into an ice sheet as further snowfalls thickened it. This fast onset of an ice age is called a *snowblitz*.

It is all to do with *albedo* and positive feedback. Albedo is a measure of reflectiveness. In hot weather we often wear light-colored clothes, and cold-weather clothes are usually dark. Pale colors are pale because they reflect most of the light falling on them. Dark colors absorb light. Light is electromagnetic radiation at wavelengths of 0.4–0.7 µm (one micron or micrometer [µm] is one-millionth of a meter, or about 0.00004 inch). Radiant heat is also electromagnetic radiation, but at wavelengths of 0.8 µm–1 millimeter (0.000003–0.04 inch). Pale colors reflect it and dark colors absorb it, just like visible light. Because of this, less heat penetrates light-colored clothes than penetrates dark ones. It makes little difference with garments as thin as a T-shirt, but much more difference with thicker clothes.

ALBEDOS

Surface	Albedo (%)
Fresh snow	75–95
Cumulus-type clouds	70–90
Stratus-type clouds	60–84
Sand (dry)	35–45
Melting or dirty snow, sea ice	30–40
Earth (average)	30
Desert	25–30
Concrete	17–27
Grass meadow	10–20
Plowed field (dry)	5–25
Asphalt	5–17
Green farm crops	3–15

Look around and you will see that the surface of the Earth varies in color. In some places it is dark, in others light, and if you have flown above the cloud tops you will know that they shine very brightly indeed. Just as with our clothes, where the Earth is dark it absorbs more heat than it does where it is light. In other words, its albedo is higher in some places than in others. Scientists have measured the albedo of different surfaces, so they can be listed according to the proportion of light and heat they reflect. The figure is given as a percentage of the total radiation falling on them, sometimes written the conventional way, as 20% for example, and sometimes as a decimal fraction, such as 0.2 (1.0 = 100%). Albedo values for some familiar surfaces are given in the table.

Water has an albedo that changes according to the angle at which light strikes the surface. When the Sun is directly overhead and the surface is still, water absorbs about 98% of the light falling on it and looks black. When the Sun is just touching the horizon, the water reflects almost all the light. Go out in a boat when the Sun is low in the sky and you can be burned by the reflected light.

As the table shows, fresh snow has a high albedo. That is why you need to wear dark glasses if you are out on a sunny day soon after it has snowed. Snow-blindness, caused by irritation of the eyes due to very bright light, can be painful.

For snow to settle, the temperature at the ground surface must remain below freezing, but snow a few inches deep will then protect the ground from the chilling effect of the wind, so air just above the surface can be up to 50° F colder than the ground beneath the snow. Heat that is reflected cannot warm the ground because it never reaches it, which means the snow does not allow the ground to warm. Nor does it prevent further gradual cooling, because the surface of the Earth radiates back into the sky almost all the solar radiation it absorbs and in winter it radiates heat it absorbed earlier in the year. You cannot manufacture snow to demonstrate its insulating effect, but white cardboard will do as well. Experiment 17 in *A Chronology of Weather* explains how you can measure the effect of albedo on the rate at which the ground warms.

Albedo can trigger temperature changes by positive *feedback*. In technical terms, feedback occurs when the output from some part of a system affects the input. When you are hungry you eat and when you have eaten enough you no longer feel hungry, so you stop eating. This is an example of feedback. In this case it is called negative feedback, because it stops the input (in this case eating) after a certain point. It would be positive feedback if it made the input continue, in this case so that the more you ate the more you wanted to go on eating. Obviously, in the natural world negative feedback is much commoner than positive feedback, but positive feedback can sometimes happen.

As winter draws to a close, the intensity of the sunlight increases. This warms the ground, which warms the air in contact with it. Snow melts and precipitation falls through the warmer air as rain rather than snow. Because even old snow reflects up to 40% of the radiation falling on it, it warms more slowly than grass or bare soil, so it melts mainly from its edges, where it is in contact with warmer ground. The snow retreats, lingering longest in sheltered places that receive little sunshine and where cold air often collects.

This is the way spring usually arrives. Suppose, though, that the winter was especially severe, with much more snow than in most years. Now suppose that the cold winter happened at a time when other factors, such as the position of the Earth in its orbital and rotational cycles (see page 41) was reducing the amount of solar radiation reaching the planet.

In high latitudes, where temperatures do not rise far above freezing even in summer, the snow might continue to reflect so much radiation that not all of the thick layer had time to melt before winter returned. More snow would fall during the next winter and the following spring the high albedo of the surface would again reflect too much radiation for all the snow to melt. By the end of the second summer the layer of surviving snow would be thicker than at the end of the first summer and probably it would cover a somewhat larger area. Year after year, the high albedo would reflect so much incoming radiation that the air above the snow remained chilled, the snow-covered area continued to spread, and the depth of snow progressively increased until its weight was sufficient to compress the lowest layer into ice.

An ice sheet would then have formed, and as the years passed it would extend into lower latitudes because once this positive feedback started its effect would be powerful. High albedo would lower the temperature, increasing the area of high-albedo snow, and causing further cooling, in a kind of vicious spiral. At this rate it might take no more than a few centuries for a full-scale ice age to become established, complete with vast ice sheets, pack ice, and valley glaciers. A century may seem a long time, but compared to the duration of an established ice age, commonly around 100,000 years, it is very brief. Change happening at this rate would be a snowblitz. Each year you would be able to measure the new area over which the ice had expanded.

No one knows whether an ice age has ever begun so rapidly. Most seem to develop gradually. Nevertheless, there seems no reason why a snowblitz could not happen, even if it has not done so until now.

Positive feedback also works in the opposite way. That is what accelerates warming when an ice age ends. Once ice sheets start to retreat, the area of exposed ground increases. Ice sheets and glaciers scour away all the soil, so at first the surface consists only of bare rock. Its albedo is around 22%, which means it absorbs 78% of the radiant heat falling on it. The rock becomes much warmer than the snow, which absorbs no more than about 60% even when it is dirty or melting, and the exposed rock will melt the snow adjacent to it. As with the snowblitz, once the process had begun, positive feedback would act as a powerful driving force.

Climates are changing constantly and in the past they have been both warmer and cooler than they are today. They are changing still. Most change is gradual and can be detected only by examining records extending over centuries, but there is no doubt that under certain circumstances positive feedback can drive a vicious spiral of rapid change.

Snow lines

High mountains are often capped with snow all year round. The lower boundary of the permanent snow cover is called the *snow line*. Climb above the snow line and you should expect blizzards at any time of year, because mountains are windy places.

As you climb, the air temperature falls. In dry air it decreases at an average rate of about 5.5° F every 1,000 feet, called the dry adiabatic lapse rate (see the box on page 62). You can work out from this that if the temperature at sea level is 59° F, which is the average over the world as a whole, anywhere above 5,000 feet the temperature will always be lower than 32° F, so even in summer precipitation will fall as snow and the snow will never melt. This is approximately correct, but in the real world the situation is more complicated.

Rain or snow, precipitation falls from air saturated with moisture, not from dry air, and in saturated air the temperature decreases more slowly with height, because the condensation of water vapor releases latent heat which warms the air. The amount of latent heat released depends on the amount of condensation and that, in turn, depends on the quantity of water vapor present in the air. This varies with the temperature of the air, warm air holding more water vapor than cold air. In other words, the saturated adiabatic lapse rate varies with air temperature. In very warm air it may be as low as 2.2° F per 1,000 feet and in very cold air it is close to the dry adiabatic lapse rate, because very cold air is also fairly dry. Where the temperature at sea level is 59° F the saturated adiabatic lapse rate is about 3° F per 1,000 feet, so in moist air the freezing temperature occurs at about 9,000 feet.

Although the sea-level temperature is usually given as 59° F, this is an average over the whole world. Obviously, the polar seas are

Figure 18: *Snow line on two sides of a mountain.*

much colder than this and tropical seas are much warmer. Indeed, near the equator sea-surface temperatures often rise above 80° F. Such warm air over the ocean is very moist, so its saturated adiabatic lapse rate may be around 2.5° F per 1,000 feet. With a starting temperature of 80° F and this lapse rate, freezing temperature is reached at just over 19,000 feet. Off the coast of Maine, on the other hand, the sea may be at about 50° F, the saturated adiabatic lapse rate about 3° F per 1,000 feet, and freezing level at 6,000 feet. Surface temperatures continue to fall with increasing distance from the equator and in very high latitudes they are below freezing through-out the year and the freezing level is at the surface, so mountains are entirely snow-covered. It is a large difference.

Much also depends on the shape and orientation of the mountain. As figure 18 shows, one side receives more sunshine than the other. This will make the snow line higher on that side. In middle latitudes, however, weather systems usually approach from the west. As the air reaches the mountain it is forced to rise. This cools it and causes its water vapor to condense and rain or snow to fall. The western side of the mountain therefore receives more precipitation than the eastern side and the snow line is likely to be lower on the exposed side, especially in shaded places.

Actual lapse rates often differ from the standard dry or saturated adiabatic lapse rate. This local lapse rate is called the environmental lapse rate. When air is forced to rise over a mountain, it cools at the standard lapse rate and this may be greater or less than the environmental lapse rate. If it is greater, by the time it reaches the summit the air may be cooler than the surrounding air. This will cause it to sink down the other side of the mountain, warming adiabatically as it does so and moving as a warm wind. Technically it is known as a Föhn wind and the best known North American example is the chinook, which blows down the eastern side of the Rocky Mountains. It is sometimes called the "snow eater" because of the rate at which it melts snow. It has been known to raise the temperature more than 40° F in two minutes and a temperature rise of 1° F a minute is quite usual. Such winds also tend to limit the amount of snow on the sheltered sides of mountains.

Real mountains are craggy, with many deep gulleys and high, projecting rock masses, so there are always shaded areas and some places in perpetual shade. Snow lingers there, but even if there could be such a thing as a perfectly smooth, conical mountain, working out which parts are most likely to be covered with snow would still be difficult. Figure 19 illustrates the problem. In middle latitudes of the northern hemisphere, the summer Sun is more or less to the southwest, so the northeastern half of the mountain is in

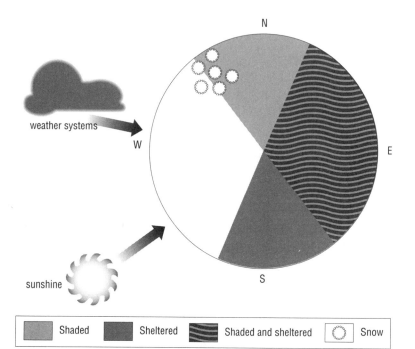

Figure 19: *Where mountain snow is most likely.*

shade, and therefore cooler. Weather systems approach from the west, so precipitation is heaviest on the western side. Combine these and, seen from above, the mountain can be divided into four unequal segments. In the south and southeast, the mountain is in full sunlight and sheltered from the weather. Between northwest and southwest it is fully exposed to the weather, but in full sunshine. Between northeast and southeast it is both shaded and sheltered, so it is cool but also dry. This leaves the north and northwest section, which is shaded but partly exposed to the weather, and it is there that snow may be expected.

In the end, there is no hard and fast rule to help you predict where the snow line will be. On average it is at about 16,000 feet in the tropics, about 8,000 feet at latitude 45° (N and S), and a little over 5,000 feet at 55°. There are mountains high enough to have snow lines in every continent. Even at the equator it is possible to experience a blizzard.

Where blizzards occur

Manitoba, Saskatchewan, and Alberta, the Canadian prairie provinces, are very cold places in winter. Temperatures often fall below -20° F and sometimes a long way below. In Edmonton, Alberta, the temperature has been known to fall below freezing in every month of the year and in January and February it can reach -57° F. Saskatoon, Saskatchewan, and Winnipeg, Manitoba, are only slightly warmer. The average January temperature in Saskatoon is -11° F, but -55° F has been recorded and -48° F has been recorded in Winnipeg.

You might suppose, therefore, that blizzards are fairly common in these places. Any precipitation must fall as snow, after all, and the prairies are certainly windy enough to drive such snow as does fall. In fact, though, blizzards are rare, especially in the coldest months, because the air is too dry. On average, less than one inch of precipitation falls each month. In fact, less snow falls in Canada than in the United States. In December, January, and February, for example, the average monthly precipitation in Winnipeg is 0.9 inch. In Chicago it is 2.0 inches. Chicago is warmer than Winnipeg, but average winter temperatures are well below freezing. Blizzards are more likely in Chicago than in Winnipeg, despite Chicago being 8° further south and markedly warmer.

Snow can fall heavily anywhere in latitudes higher than about 30° but, far from being confined to the Arctic, blizzards are less common in very high latitudes than they are in warmer regions. This is because snow cannot fall at all unless the air is saturated, and at temperatures below about 4° F, air can hold barely enough water vapor to produce any precipitation at all. When it is really cold, with temperatures well below freezing, the sky is usually clear, with barely a cloud to be seen. It is not extremely cold air that brings blizzards, but relatively warm air. Snow is most likely when the air temperature is between 25° F and 39° F. Then the air holds enough moisture to produce precipitation, but the temperature below the cloud is low enough to prevent the snow from melting before it reaches the ground.

These conditions are most likely to occur at the beginning and end of winter, which is when blizzards are most likely. There is often heavy snow around or shortly before Thanksgiving. In 1980, there were snowstorms along the whole eastern side of the United States northward from New Mexico on November 17 and 18, and there were severe winter storms around the Great Lakes on November 8, 1913 and November 10, 1975. Spring blizzards often happen in March. There were especially severe storms from March 11 to 14, 1888 that brought an average 40 inches of snow to New England and part of New York State and caused more than 400 deaths. This is only a general rule, of course, and there are many exceptions. The 1996 blizzards over most of the eastern United States, and also in Britain, occurred in January, and in 1888, one of the harshest

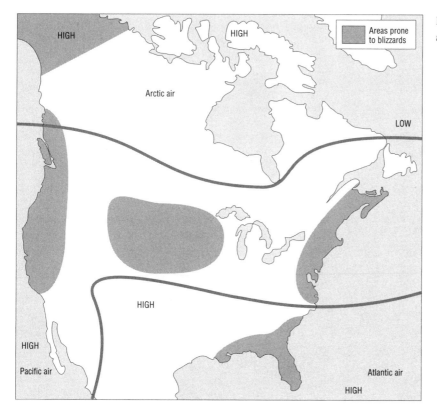

Figure 20: *Winter air masses in North America.*

The Coriolis effect

Any object moving toward or away from the equator and not firmly attached to the surface does not travel in a straight line. It is deflected to the right in the northern hemisphere and to the left in the southern hemisphere. Moving air and water tend to follow a clockwise path in the northern hemisphere and a counterclockwise path in the southern hemisphere.

The reason for this was discovered in 1835 by the French physicist Gaspard Gustave de Coriolis and it is called the *Coriolis effect*. It happens because the Earth is a rotating sphere and as an object moves above the surface, the Earth below is also moving. The effect used to be called the Coriolis *force*, but it is not a force. It results simply from the fact that we observe motion in relation to fixed points on the surface. The effect is easily demonstrated by the simple experiment (2) described in *A Chronology of Weather*.

The Coriolis effect.

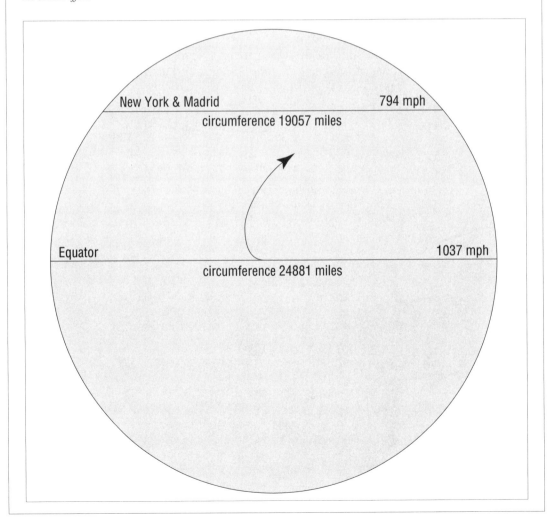

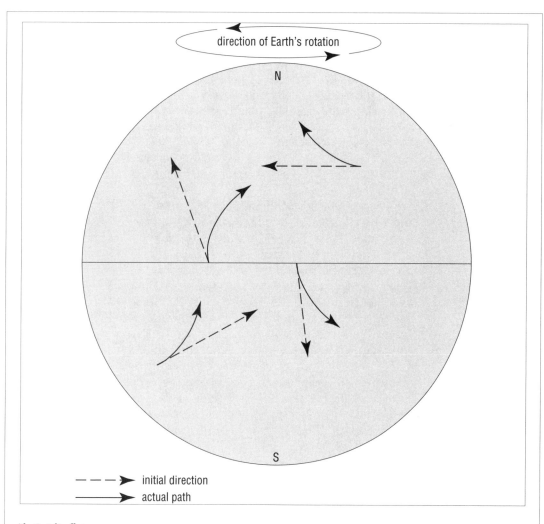

direction of Earth's rotation

N

S

— — — ▸ initial direction
————▸ actual path

The Coriolis effect.

The Earth makes one complete turn on its axis every 24 hours. This means every point on the surface is constantly moving and returns to its original position (relative to the Sun) every 24 hours, but different points on the surface travel different distances to do so. Consider two points on the surface, one at the equator and the other at 40° N, which is the approximate latitude of New York and Madrid. The equator, latitude 0°, is about 24,881 miles long. That is how far a point on the equator must travel in 24 hours, which means it moves at about 1,037 MPH. At 40° N, the circumference parallel to the equator is about 19,057 miles. The point there has less distance to travel and so it moves at about 794 MPH.

Suppose you planned to fly an aircraft to New York from the point on the equator due south of New York (and you could ignore the winds). If you headed due north you would not reach New York. At the equator you are already traveling eastward at 1,037 MPH. As you fly north, the surface beneath you is also traveling east, but at a slower speed the farther you travel. If the journey from 0° to 40° N took you six hours, in that time you would also move about 6,000 miles to the east, relative to the position of the surface beneath you, but the surface itself would also move, at New York by about 4,700 miles, so you would end not at New York, but (6,000 - 4,700 =) 1,300 miles to the east of New York, way out over the Atlantic.

The size of the Coriolis effect is directly proportional to the speed at which the body moves and the sine of its latitude. The effect on a body moving at 100 MPH is ten times greater than that on one moving at 10 MPH, and the Coriolis effect is greatest at the poles and zero at the equator.

winters on record, Montana, the Dakotas, and Minnesota suffered the worst blizzards they had ever known from January 11 to 13.

In winter, as figure 20 shows, three types of air affect North America. Arctic air, covering most of Canada, is dry and air spills south from the polar high-pressure region at its center. The Caribbean, Gulf of Mexico, and southeastern United States lie beneath mild, moist air from the Atlantic. Between these, the western coastal region and a broad band across the central United States are affected by air from the Pacific. Associated with these, pressure is usually low over to the east of Greenland and high over the Arctic, central United States, and over the sea off California and the southern Caribbean. The Pacific and Caribbean high-pressure areas are much farther south and exert less influence than in summer and in the belt of Pacific air, moving generally eastward across the continent, air masses of different types are mixing to produce frontal systems (see the box on page 14).

Typically, a weather system that brings blizzards to eastern North America starts off the coast of the Carolinas as an area of low pressure. It intensifies, so the winds circulating around it increase in strength (see page 58), and moves north, to the position shown in figure 20. The winds flow counterclockwise because of the Coriolis effect (see box on page 52) and figure 21 shows the consequences. The winds blow across the ocean, gathering moisture, and reach the east coast blowing from the east. As the low moves north these winds cause floods and erode beaches, but by the time they reach New England they also bring heavy snow and blizzards.

Further south, cold, continental polar air occasionally pushes across Texas as far as the Gulf and Florida. It can bring blizzards. More commonly, cold air advancing from the north meets warmer air from the Gulf. Cold air undercuts the warm air, lifting it and causing its moisture vapor to condense. The resulting rain turns to snow as it falls through the underlying layer of cold air, producing fierce storms, with blizzards, across the midwest.

Along the west coast, storms developing in moist Pacific air produce blizzards as they reach the coast. Cold air is funneled through mountain valleys as it crosses the Rockies and wind speeds

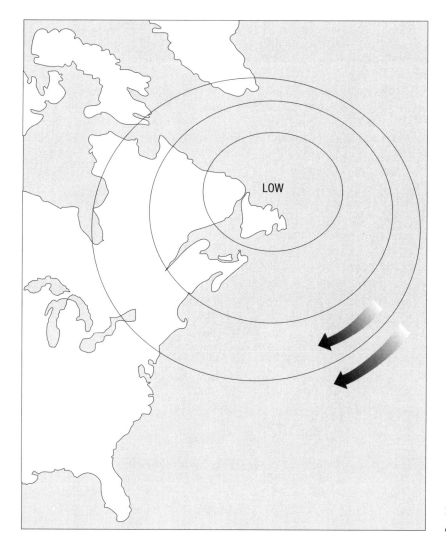

Figure 21: *Wind direction around a winter low.*

can reach 100 MPH. Alaska suffers from fierce storms moving eastward from the Bering Sea. Not only do these cause blizzards, their winds can hurl huge blocks of sea ice onto the shore with enough force to damage any buildings they hit.

Western Europe receives most of its weather systems from the Atlantic. In winter these can bring deep areas of low pressure (depressions) with strong winds and heavy precipitation that falls as snow in the north. The deep interior of the continental land mass is very dry, however, and even in Siberia snowfall is light. In winter the relative humidity is often higher than 85%, but the air is so cold that very little water vapor is needed to saturate it. A relative humidity of 88% at an air temperature of -6° F is equivalent to a relative humidity of 6% at a temperature of 60° F.

For most of the time, Siberian winters are pleasant. Despite the cold, the sky is blue, the air calm, and the sunshine is bright enough to melt snow. Siberia does experience blizzards, of course. In the tundra regions of the north, the wind producing blizzards is called the *purga*. Farther south, along the southern border of the belt of conifer forest known as the *taiga* and into Mongolia and Manchuria, it is called the *buran*. The wind blows, from the northeast, when continental polar air is drawn into the area behind a depression. It carries falling snow, lifts lying snow, and quickly builds to hurricane force (more than 75 MPH). It is a terrifying phenomenon, and very dangerous to anyone exposed to it.

Blizzards are more common in some places than in others, but this should not lull you into a false sense of security, no matter where you live. They are possible wherever snow falls and strong winds blow, even on mountains in the tropics. Where people expect blizzards they are prepared for them and know what to do. It is where they are unexpected that they are likely to cause most harm. In February 1973, snowstorms and blizzards closed highways, disrupted communications, and caused chaos in Georgia and the Carolinas, mainly because people had so little experience of such severe conditions. Nowhere can claim to be totally immune and it is wise to be prepared.

Gales and why they happen

When it is snowing heavily, any wind stronger than 35 MPH will turn a snowstorm into a blizzard. Even if the sky is cloudless, a wind of this force can lift freshly fallen snow from the ground. Once airborne, the snow will be driven by the wind just like falling snow. Again, the result is a blizzard.

A wind of 32–38 MPH is known technically as a *moderate gale*. Winds stronger than this are called *fresh gale*, *strong gale*, *whole gale*, and *storm*. When the wind speed exceeds 75 MPH the wind is a hurricane. We still classify wind strength according to a method worked out nearly two centuries ago by a British admiral (see box on page 58). He named each type of wind and gave it a *force number* between 0 and 12. On his scale a moderate gale is a force 7 wind.

Admiral Beaufort described winds, but his scale does not explain why winds vary in strength or, indeed, why they happen at all. They are due to differences in air pressure.

Stand in a strong wind and you can feel its pressure. It pushes against you. Anything that can push you around must be a material substance and a material substance has weight. If you doubt that air has weight, experiment 18 in *A Chronology of Weather* should convince you.

Imagine a circle drawn on the ground. Above that circle there is a column of air reaching all the way to the top of the atmosphere. The weight of all that air is pushing downward on the ground within the circle and the force exerted by that weight is measured as air pressure.

Now suppose there are two imaginary circles, both the same size but one in a very warm place and the other in a very cold place. Contact with the ground will warm the air, so one column of air will be warm and the other cold. When molecules absorb heat its energy makes them move faster and further away from one another. This means the column of warm air contains fewer air molecules than the column of cold air. Experiment 4 in *A Chronology of Weather* demonstrates the effect of changing temperature on a volume of air. If one column contains fewer molecules than the other it must weigh less, because its molecules are what makes air (or anything else) a material substance at all, so it will exert less pressure on the surface. The air pressure inside one circle will be lower than that inside the other. In the real world, it is local differences in air pressure that produce our weather.

Inflate a balloon and it is the air pressure inside that stretches the rubber. Once inflated, the air pressure is greater inside the balloon than it is outside. Release the balloon, or burst it, and the

Figure 22: *Known as "Home of the World's Worst Weather," the Mount Washington Observatory is located at the summit of the tallest mountain in the northeastern United States. The highest wind velocity ever recorded at a surface station, 231 MPH, was measured there on April 12, 1934. In this photograph, a member of the team de-ices tower instruments.* (Courtesy of the Mount Washington Observatory)

air will escape. It will flow from the region of high pressure inside to the region of low pressure outside, and it will do so with some force. Air moves out of areas of high pressure into areas of low pressure and the force with which it does so is proportional to the difference between the high and low pressures. You can think of this difference as a slope, or gradient, down which the air flows. If there is a large pressure difference and the centers of high and low pressure are close together, the gradient will be steep. If they are far apart, or the difference in pressure is small, the gradient will be shallow. The force moving the air is called the *pressure-gradient force*, or PGF.

While it remains inside the balloon, the air is confined by the balloon itself and without the balloon the pressure difference would

Wind force and Admiral Beaufort

In 1806, the Royal Navy issued a scale by which sailors could estimate the strength of the wind by observing its effects. The scale also instructed them on the amount of sail appropriate to each wind strength.

The scale had been devised by Admiral Sir Francis Beaufort (see *A Chronology of Weather* for a biographical note) and is still known as the Beaufort scale. Eventually it was adopted internationally.

The Beaufort scale classifies winds into 13 named *forces* (in 1955 meteorologists at the United States Weather Bureau added five more to describe hurricane-force winds). Wind speeds were originally given in knots, the unit often still used by ships and aircraft. In the scale given here, knots have been converted to miles per hour and rounded to the nearest whole number. (1 knot = 1 nautical mile per hour = 1.15 MPH.)

Force 0. 1 MPH or less. Calm. The air feels still and smoke rises vertically.

Force 1. 1–3 MPH. Light air. Wind vanes and flags do not move, but rising smoke drifts.

Force 2. 4–7 MPH. Light breeze. Drifting smoke indicates the wind direction.

Force 3. 8–12 MPH. Gentle breeze. Leaves rustle, small twigs move, and flags made from lightweight material stir gently.

Force 4. 13–18 MPH. Moderate breeze. Loose leaves and pieces of paper blow about.

Force 5. 19–24 MPH. Fresh breeze. Small trees that are in full leaf wave in the wind.

Force 6. 25–31 MPH. Strong breeze. It becomes difficult to use an open umbrella.

Force 7. 32–38 MPH. Moderate gale. The wind exerts strong pressure on people walking into it.

Force 8. 39–46 MPH. Fresh gale. Small twigs are torn from trees.

Force 9. 47–54 MPH. Strong gale. Chimneys blown down, slates and tiles torn from roofs.

Force 10. 55–63 MPH. Whole gale. Trees are broken or uprooted.

Force 11. 64–75 MPH. Storm. Trees are uprooted and blown some distance. Cars are overturned.

Force 12. More than 75 MPH. Hurricane. Devastation is widespread. Buildings are destroyed, many trees uprooted. In the original instruction, "no sail can stand."

not arise. Simply blowing into the air has no effect on air pressure. You might wonder, therefore, how pressure differences can develop in the atmosphere, where there are no balloons to help. You might suppose air would move around freely, equalizing pressures before gradients could form, in which case wind would be impossible.

Gradients form because air does not flow in straight lines. Instead of moving directly from a center of high pressure to a center of low pressure it follows an almost circular path at right angles to the pressure gradient. In 1857, the Dutch meteorologist Christoph Buys Ballot found that in the northern hemisphere air flows counterclockwise around centers of low pressure and clockwise around centers of high pressure. This became known as *Buys Ballot's law* (see box on page 60).

The law is a consequence of the combined effect of the pressure-gradient force (PGF) and the Coriolis effect, or CorF (see box on page 52). Figure 23 shows the result.

As the air flows, the CorF, acting at right angles to the direction of flow, swings it to the right in the northern hemisphere and to the left in the southern hemisphere. As it starts to swing to the right, the CorF and PGF produce a resultant force that accelerates it. CorF is proportional to the speed of the moving air, so it increases, swinging the air still more to the right. This continues until the air is flowing parallel to the isobars (lines joining places of equal atmospheric pressure) and, therefore, at right angles to the pressure gradient. At this point, the PGF and CorF are acting in opposite directions. If the PGF is the stronger, the air will swing to the left and accelerate. This will increase the CorF, swinging it back to the right again. If the CorF is the stronger, the air will swing farther to the right, the PGF acting in the opposite direction will slow it, the CorF will decrease, and the air will swing to the left again.

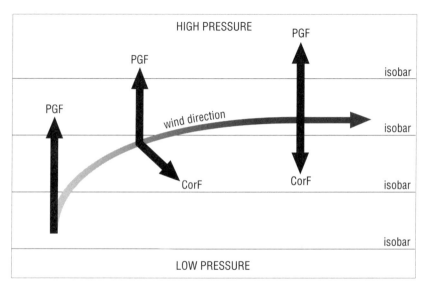

Figure 23: *How the geostrophic wind is produced.*

Christoph Buys Ballot and his law

In 1857, the Dutch meteorologist Christoph Buys Ballot (see *Chronology* for a biographical note) published a summary of his observations on the relationship between atmospheric pressure and wind. He had concluded that in the northern hemisphere winds flow counterclockwise around areas of low pressure and clockwise around areas of high pressure. In the southern hemisphere these directions are reversed.

Unknown to Buys Ballot, a few months earlier the American meteorologist William Ferrel had applied the laws of physics and calculated this would be the case. Buys Ballot acknowledged Ferrel's prior claim to the discovery, but despite this, the phenomenon is now known as *Buys Ballot's law*. This states that, in the northern hemisphere, if you stand with your back to the wind the area of low pressure is to your left and the area of high pressure to your right. In the southern hemisphere, if you stand with your back to the wind the area of low pressure is to your right and the area of high pressure to your left. (The law does not apply very close to the equator.)

Buys Ballot's law.

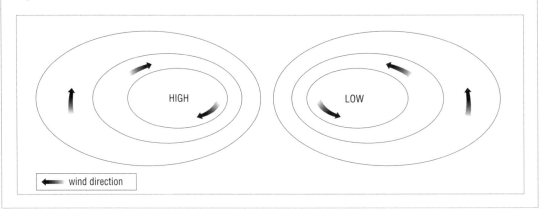

Near the ground, friction with the surface and objects on it slows the air, acting as an additional force. This deflects the air so it flows at an angle to the isobars, rather than parallel to them, allowing pressures to equalize. Clear of the surface, the air does flow parallel to the isobars. This is called the *geostrophic wind.*

Wind consists of air set in motion by a pressure gradient and flowing approximately at right angles to it. The strength of the wind depends on the steepness of the pressure gradient and you can work this out by looking at a weather map that shows the isobars. The closer together the isobars are, the steeper the gradient and, therefore, the stronger the wind. Isobars are very like the contours on an ordinary map. Closely packed contours indicate a steep slope (gradient) and closely packed isobars indicate a steep pressure gradient.

Calculating the actual wind force is more complicated. This also depends on the density of the moving air, which in turn depends on its temperature, and relating all the factors involves some advanced mathematics. All the same, when you see a weather map with isobars closely packed together you can be sure it means strong winds. When you see such a weather map in winter, when the surface air temperature is close to freezing, the next thing to look for in the forecast is precipitation. If weather fronts (see box on page 14) are shown on the map precipitation is likely (but not inevitable, because some fronts are weak) and it will fall as snow. Driven by winds greater than force 7, heavy snow will turn into a blizzard. Even if no snowfall is forecast, the packed isobars may mean recent falls will be lifted by the wind. Either way the result will be a blizzard. It pays to keep an eye on winter weather maps.

Hail, sleet, snow

Snow is frozen water, but not all frozen water falling from clouds is snow. Ice can also fall as hail and even the word *snow* is somewhat vague. There are many kinds of snow (see page 74).

Whether water falls from a cloud as fog, rain, drizzle, sleet, snow, or hail depends partly on what is happening inside the cloud, but also on what happens to the falling water after it leaves the cloud. Not all the water that falls reaches the ground at all. Wait for a day, in any season of the year, when there are light showers. These fall from puffy, white or gray cumulus clouds. Look at those in the distance and beneath some of them you may see what appears to be a kind of gray veil. It has the same appearance as a distant shower, but showers reach all the way to the ground and this veil extends only part of the way. It is called *virga*, and it is exactly what it looks like: a shower that fails to reach the ground, because its water droplets evaporate before they can do so.

Rising air cools adiabatically (see box on page 4) and the lower its temperature the less water vapor it can hold. Beyond a certain height, therefore, the air will become saturated and water vapor will start to condense into liquid droplets. This is how clouds form (see box on page 62), the type of cloud varying according to the vigor with which the air rises.

Below the cloud the relative humidity of the air is less than 100%. This air is not saturated. Inside the cloud the air is saturated. We know the division between the two layers of air is quite sharp because clouds have clearly defined bases, although if you fly just beneath clouds you can see that they are rather wispier than they look from the ground. When water falls from the base of a cloud it enters unsaturated air and so it starts to evaporate.

What happens next depends on the water. When a droplet of water falls through the air, its weight pulls it downward, but the air

Evaporation, condensation, and the formation of clouds

When air rises it cools adiabatically, by an average of 5.5° F every 1,000 feet. This is called the *dry adiabatic lapse rate*. Moving air may be forced to rise if it crosses high ground, such as a mountain or mountain range, or meets a mass of cooler, denser air at a front. Locally, air may also rise by convection where the ground is warmed unevenly.

There will be a height, called the *condensation level*, at which the temperature of the air falls to its dew point. As the air rises above this level the water vapor it contains will start to condense. Condensation releases latent heat, warming the air. After the relative humidity of the air reaches 100% and the air continues to rise, it will cool at the saturated adiabatic lapse rate of about 3° F per 1,000 feet.

Water vapor will condense at a relative humidity as low as 78% if the air contains minute particles of a substance that readily dissolves in water. Salt crystals and sulfate particles are common examples. If the air contains insoluble particles, such as dust, the vapor will condense at about 100% relative humidity. If there are no particles at all, the relative humidity may exceed 100% and the air will be supersaturated, although the relative humidity in clouds rarely exceeds 101%.

The particles on to which water vapor condenses are called *cloud condensation nuclei* (CCN). They range in size from 0.001 µm to more than 10 µm diameter; water will condense onto the smallest particles only if the air is strongly supersaturated and the largest particles are so heavy they do not remain airborne very long. Condensation is most efficient on CCN averaging 0.2 µm diameter (1 µm = one-millionth of a meter = 0.00004 inches).

At first, water droplets vary in size according to the size of the nuclei onto which they condensed. After that, the droplets grow but also lose water by evaporation because they are warmed by the latent heat of condensation. Some freeze, grow into snowflakes, and then melt as they fall into a lower, warmer region of the cloud. Others grow as large droplets collide and merge with smaller ones.

Cloud formation.

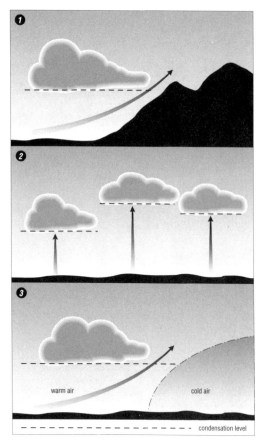

warm air   cold air

— — — — — — — — — — — — — — — — condensation level

resists its movement. Try to wave a sheet of paper through the air quickly and the paper will curve back because of the resistance offered by the air. The speed at which a droplet falls increases until the downward force of its weight balances the resistance of the air, acting as an upward force (called *drag*). After that the droplet no longer accelerates. It has attained its *terminal velocity*.

Not all droplets reach the same terminal velocity. This is because the weight of an object is proportional to its volume, but drag acts on its surface area, and the greater the volume of a body the more surface area it has in proportion. This sounds strange, but it is a matter of geometry. Suppose, for example, that a spherical water droplet has a radius of 4 (the units do not matter). Its volume (given by the equation $4/3\pi r^3$) is 268 and its surface area ($4\pi r^2$) is 201. To work out how much surface area there is for each unit of volume, divide the surface area by the volume (201 ÷ 268) and the answer is 0.75. Now imagine a droplet half as big, with a radius of 2. Its volume will be 33.5, its surface area 50.3, and for each unit of its volume it will have 1.5 units of surface area (33.5 ÷ 50.3). The bigger the droplet, the more it weighs in proportion to its surface area and, therefore, the greater its terminal velocity will be. Drizzle feels gentle because it falls slowly, with a terminal velocity of around 2.5 feet per second. Rain, with much bigger drops, falls at 13 to more than 30 feet per second.

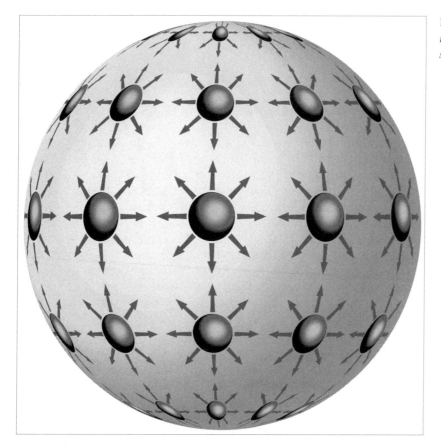

Figure 24: *Surface tension: why water droplets are spherical.*

Up to a point ice behaves in the same way as liquid water. Although it is slightly less dense than very cold water, this makes no difference to its weight-to-drag ratio because both ice and liquid water are about 1,000 times denser than air. What does make a difference is its shape.

Liquid water tends to form spherical droplets. It does so because of *surface tension.* As figure 24 shows, water molecules attract one another with a force acting equally in all directions. At the surface, however, there is a layer of molecules with no water molecules attracting them from above. These are held by the attraction of molecules to the side and below. If the water is in contact with nothing except air, this attraction will pull it into a spherical shape. Only liquids experience surface tension. Ice is solid and its shape is determined by the way it forms. It may form approximately spherical blocks, like hail, but it can also assume the delicate shapes of snowflakes.

A sphere has a smaller surface area in relation to its volume than any other shape. A volume of 8 cubic inches can be enclosed by a cube with a total surface area of 24 square inches, for example, but a sphere enclosing the same volume has a surface area of only 19.35 square inches.

Increase the surface area of a falling object and the drag also increases. Increase the surface area in relation to the volume, and therefore the weight, and its terminal velocity will decrease. In other words, a spherical hailstone will fall at the same speed as a water droplet of the same weight, but ice with any shape other than spherical will fall more slowly. There are two consequences of this. The first is that snowflakes drift down very gently. Depending on their size and precise shape they fall at about 1 or 2 feet per second. The second consequence is that once hailstones grow larger than an average raindrop they fall faster, at 25 feet per second or more, and giant hailstones, nearly one inch in diameter, fall at around 65 feet per second, which is fast enough to injure anyone hit by them and to damage farm crops and the roofs of buildings.

Big droplets fall faster than small droplets, but this does not apply to the smallest droplets of all. These weigh so little that their movement is entirely governed by the stronger motion of the air around them. This is why cloud droplets remain inside their clouds until they have collided with others, coalesced with them, and grown to a size large enough for them to start falling.

Once it leaves its cloud, a water droplet enters unsaturated air and starts evaporating. This makes it grow smaller, altering its volume-to-surface area ratio and slowing its fall. The more slowly it falls the longer it remains in the air and so the more it will evaporate. This sets a limit on the distance a water droplet of any particular size can fall before it evaporates altogether. If it is to reach the ground from a height of 1,000 feet or so, a water droplet must leave the cloud with a radius no smaller than about 100 µm (about 0.004 inch) and, even so, the air below the cloud must be close to saturation. Droplets of this size reach the ground as drizzle.

Cloud droplets are no more than 20 µm (0.0008 inch) in diameter, one-tenth the size of drizzle droplets. Some of them do fall from their cloud, but travel only an inch or two before they evaporate. They make the bottom of the cloud wispy when seen at close quarters, but sharp when seen from a distance.

Ice crystals will form inside a cloud provided the air temperature is below freezing. It often happens that the upper part of a cloud is below freezing, but the lower part is not. Ice forms near the top, but as the crystals fall they melt and precipitation falls as rain. Even if precipitation leaves a cloud as ice crystals, these will melt if they have to fall very far through air at above freezing temperature. To fall as snow, the temperature must usually be at freezing below about 1,000 feet.

If the temperature in the lower part of the cloud is close to freezing, precipitation will leave it as very cold water droplets. They will remain liquid if the temperature is above freezing in the air beneath the cloud, but if this air is just below freezing temperature some or all of the droplets will freeze. They may fall as tiny crystals, much the same size as drizzle droplets. These will not stick to objects and usually they bounce when they strike a hard surface. In North America this is known as *sleet*. In Britain, sleet is a mixture of snow and rain falling together.

Bigger snowflakes need cloud temperatures below freezing throughout. This allows ice crystals to combine without melting, and snowflakes form best in cloud temperatures of 32° F down to 23° F. Then they must fall through air beneath the cloud that is also below freezing temperature, although it may be warmer than the air inside the cloud. The size of snowflakes depends largely on the movement of the air. If the air moves vigorously, the flakes are broken apart before they can grow very large, but in very calm air flakes can reach an inch or more across. These are the flakes that cling to surfaces. If you walk through falling snow of this kind, before long your coat and hat are covered in it. It is the shape of its crystals that make it cling so firmly (see page 74).

Snow may also fall as tiny pellets. These are white, often roughly spherical or conical in shape, and most are no more than one-tenth of an inch across. Many are smaller. Their white color is due to the fact that they are composed of individual ice crystals loosely joined together with air spaces between them, rather like tiny, folded-up snowflakes. This structure also makes them soft. Being so small, they fall slowly, but even so they are often smashed when they strike hard ground. These pellets are called *soft hail*, or *graupel* (from the German word for sleet). They form in clouds containing little liquid water. Water vapor freezes directly onto them. If, as they fall, they enter a region where the temperature is above freezing and water is abundant, water may freeze onto them as a layer of clear ice. Ice pellets may also fall if raindrops freeze or snowflakes melt and then freeze again.

True hail is different. It forms in storms that are moving across the surface, steered by a strong wind at high level. A hailstone begins as a rain droplet. Ordinarily it would be heavy enough to fall from the cloud, but instead it is carried aloft by strong upcurrents. High in the cloud, the water freezes and the raindrop becomes a small sphere of ice. Near the top of the cloud it is swept forward by the high-level wind. Then it starts to fall. As it falls, it passes through tiny droplets of water chilled to below freezing temperature. These supercooled liquid droplets freeze instantly as the hailstone touches them, forming a layer of white rime ice. As it falls further, the hailstone enters a part of the cloud where the water content is higher, but there are still many supercooled droplets. These also freeze on contact, but spread as they do so, forming a layer of clear ice. By this time, the advancing storm has caught up with the falling hailstone. It enters the upcurrents and is carried aloft again. This happens repeatedly, producing a layered structure. If you could slice a big hailstone in half, you would see that it is made up of layers, like an onion. The layers are alternately white and clear, each pair of layers made up from white rime ice covered by a layer of clear ice.

Its outer layer of clear ice gives a hailstone its strength. When it hits the ground it does not shatter, it bounces. Its size depends on the number of times it has made its *accretion circuit*, of being carried to the top of the cloud, dropped, and carried aloft again, acquiring another pair of layers with each round trip. Most hailstones are quite small, seldom growing to more than about one-quarter of an inch across, but in really huge, violent clouds they can become much larger.

Water vapor can change directly into ice, and ice directly into vapor, without passing through a liquid phase. This is called *sublimation*. You may have seen it happen, when patches of snow shrink or disappear even though the temperature is well below freezing. The ice crystals have sublimed into dry air.

Tiny ice crystals can fall from even a cloudless sky if the air is cold enough and contains freezing nuclei. Water vapor sublimes directly into ice, rather than condensing into liquid droplets. The resulting crystals sometimes glitter in the sunlight and are known as "diamond dust."

Some consequences of supercooling are attractive and harmless. Freezing fog and freezing rain are less pleasant.

Freezing rain and freezing fog

As air cools, its capacity for holding water vapor decreases and, therefore, its relative humidity increases. When the relative humidity reaches 100% the air is saturated, and ordinarily water vapor will start to condense into liquid droplets as the air approaches saturation.

In order to condense, however, tiny solid particles must be present to which water molecules can attach themselves (see box on page 62). Dust, smoke, salt, and sulfur dioxide are among the substances with particles onto which water vapor will condense. These are called *condensation nuclei* and most air contains plenty of them. Over land, there are 300–400 of them in every cubic inch of air and over the oceans, far from any source of dust, there are about 60 in every cubic inch. In really clean air water vapor is more reluctant to condense. The air becomes supersaturated and under laboratory conditions its relative humidity can be increased to more than 300% before droplets form spontaneously. Natural air is never this clean, but air is often supersaturated by 1 or 2%. Experiment 19 in *Chronology* shows how easy it is for clouds to form when ordinary air is made to expand and cools adiabatically even slightly.

Just as condensation nuclei must be present before water vapor will condense out of saturated air, so freezing nuclei must be present before water droplets will freeze at low temperature. Freezing nuclei are much rarer than condensation nuclei and the colder the air the fewer of them there are. Air seldom contains more than 0.06 of them per cubic inch and at around -20° F there may be fewer than 0.0006 per cubic inch (approximately one nucleus in every 1,700 cubic inches of air). Fine soil particles are common freezing nuclei and volcanic dust and chemical compounds released by plants may also contribute, but once ice crystals have started forming they encourage water to freeze onto them.

Even in the presence of freezing nuclei, airborne water droplets do not turn into ice the moment the temperature falls below 32° F. At 15° F a cloud still consists almost entirely of water droplets. As the temperature falls below -4° F ice crystals increase to outnumber the water droplets, but it is not until the temperature falls below -20° F that clouds consist wholly of ice crystals and even then there are exceptions. In the absence of freezing nuclei, water droplets can be cooled to -40° F before they freeze spontaneously.

Water that has been chilled below freezing temperature is said to be *supercooled*, and supercooled cloud droplets are very common. Temperatures are below freezing in most big clouds, even in summer. In saturated air, in which water vapor is condensing, if the temperature at ground level is 80° F, air will be at freezing temperature (32° F) at 16,000 feet. In winter, when the ground-level temperature is, say, 30° F, it will be 20° F at about 3,000 feet. Even in summer, much of the rain that falls in middle latitudes is snow that has melted during its descent.

At just below 32° F, water on the ground will start to freeze. Ice will appear around the edges of ponds and over puddles. Cloud droplets at this temperature are still liquid and most of them will remain so at much lower temperatures. They are still able to form raindrops, so it is quite possible for rain to be composed of water at below freezing temperature. For most of the year it will fall through warmer air beneath its cloud, so by the time it reaches the ground it will have warmed to above freezing, although it may still feel cold on your face and hands.

It is in winter that it can cause problems. The air temperature beneath the cloud is usually higher than that inside the cloud, but it may still be a degree or two below freezing. The supercooled raindrops are warmed as they fall, but not to a temperature above freezing. They fall as *freezing rain*.

Any solid object will act as a freezing nucleus and the rain will freeze on contact with it. Freezing is almost instantaneous, but it affects only the water in contact with the surface. As each raindrop strikes, the first part of the drop freezes and supercooled water behind it spills to the sides, freezing as it reaches the surface. Each drop freezes into a thin film of ice and a shower of rain coats everything on which it falls with a layer of clear ice. Freezing rain turns roads and sidewalks into skating rinks and makes walking and driving hazardous.

When the ground-level temperature is low enough, the raindrops do not need to be supercooled to produce freezing rain. It sometimes happens that a layer of warm air lies above a layer of cooler air. Temperature usually decreases with height, so this is called a *temperature inversion*. Rain may fall from a cloud in the inversion layer. It will be a degree or two above freezing temperature, but the air beneath it is cooler, a few degrees below freezing, and the ground and objects near the ground will be at the same temperature as the cooler air. As the falling raindrops strike, they will be chilled by contact with the surface and will freeze onto it. Again, a layer of clear ice will form very quickly.

Freezing rain is distinguished only by the fact that it freezes on contact with a surface. The rain itself can be of any type. It may be a shower, with large drops, or more prolonged drizzle. In either case it coats everything with clear ice, the thickness of the ice depending only on the amount of rain that falls.

Water vapor condenses when air is cooled, but there are several ways to cool air and some of them cause condensation at ground level. This is fog, composed of minute droplets identical to those in cloud. Indeed, sometimes fog is cloud. If moist air rises as it crosses high ground, adiabatic cooling may make cloud form before the air reaches the top. Hill walkers often find themselves in fog that is really cloud.

Warm, moist air may also drift over cold ground. The horizontal movement of heat is called *advection*. As the air is chilled by contact with the ground beneath it, its water vapor may condense to form *advection fog*.

The third common cause of fog is radiation, and it is called *radiation fog*. During the day the ground is warmed by the Sun and at night it radiates away the heat it received, so it cools rapidly. If the air above it is clear, but close to saturation, the ground may cool sufficiently to cause low-level condensation in the early hours of the morning and by dawn there will be fog.

The temperature to which air must be cooled to reach saturation, so water vapor condenses, is called its *dew point*. Obviously, this varies according to the amount of water vapor present in the air, so the drier the air the lower its dew-point temperature. It can happen that the dew-point temperature is below freezing. In this case, water vapor will not condense into liquid droplets, but sublime directly into ice crystals. At night, heat radiated from the surface may lower the temperature to below the dew-point temperature of the air in contact with it. Water vapor will then condense as dew, but if the dew-point temperature is below freezing and the ground cools sufficiently it will deposit ice crystals on all exposed surfaces. In the morning you will see them as frost. It is the ice drivers must scrape from their windshields before they can set off on their travels.

Suppose, though, that the air is rather moister than this, so its dew-point temperature is above freezing. As it is chilled from below, fog will form. If the ground, and objects on the ground, are much colder than freezing, the fog will freeze onto exposed surfaces. This produces rime ice. Air trapped among the ice crystals makes it white and because it forms from the freezing of individual, tiny droplets of liquid, it has an uneven texture.

Freezing will be especially rapid if the fog consists of supercooled droplets, which it may be if the air is chilled in stages. First it is cooled to below its dew-point temperature, so liquid droplets form. Then it is cooled further, to below 32° F, and the droplets become supercooled. They will now freeze instantly onto any surface at a temperature below freezing.

This is called *freezing fog* and, although it is not so dangerous as freezing rain, it can cause serious difficulties, especially for drivers. After it has stood in the open for a short time, the exterior of a car is at the same temperature as the air. As it travels, the airflow over it carries away any heat warming it from inside the vehicle. You may be warm inside the car, with the heater on, but the outside of the car is cold. If you drive through freezing fog, it will freeze instantly on contact with the windshield and the defogger will be no help. It only warms the inside of the glass to evaporate condensation from air inside the car. With ordinary fog the wipers will clear droplets from the windshield, but in freezing fog they merely spread them into a film of white ice. Meanwhile, while the driver struggles to see the road ahead through this film of ice, droplets may also be freezing onto the road surface, so the road is acquiring a coating of ice.

When freezing rain or freezing fog are forecast, motoring organizations and the police advise drivers to stay at home. You should attempt only really essential journeys in such conditions.

What happens when water freezes and ice melts

Water is one of the most common substances on our planet. It is also the most remarkable, and if water did not possess some extremely peculiar properties our weather would be very different.

At the range of temperatures found over the surface of our planet and in the lower atmosphere, water exists as a gas, liquid, and solid, often as all three in the same area. This is its first peculiarity. With most substances, the smaller the molecules from which they are made, the lower their freezing and boiling temperatures. Water molecules, comprising one atom of oxygen and two of hydrogen, are quite small. Hydrochloric acid (HCl), for example, melts at about -174° F and boils at -121° F, ozone (O_3) melts at -315° F and boils at -167° F, and nitrous oxide (N_2O) melts at -131° F and boils at -127° F. These substances have molecules comparable in size to that of water. Based on molecule size alone, we would expect ice to melt at around -148° F and water to boil at around -112° F. If it did, there would be very little liquid water on Earth and no ice at all. Water would exist only as vapor. Rain would be impossible and everywhere would be desert in which nothing at all could live.

Again, the density of most substances increases as they are cooled because their molecules pack together more closely, and this continues until they turn into solids. Water does increase in density as it cools, but only slightly, and fresh water reaches its maximum density while still a liquid. Ice is less dense than liquid water, which is why it floats. If this were not so, ice forming over lakes and ponds, not to mention the oceans, would sink to the bottom, which would be highly inconvenient for aquatic life.

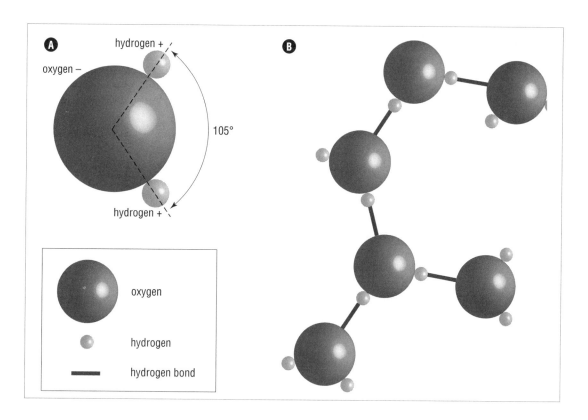

Both of these properties are due to the structure of the water molecule itself. A molecule is composed of atoms, in the case of water two of hydrogen and one of oxygen, usually written as H_2O. An atom comprises a nucleus, with a positive electric charge, surrounded by a cloud of electrons with a negative electric charge. The charges usually balance, so the atom as a whole possesses no overall charge (but if an atom loses or gains electrons it will acquire a charge, in which case it is said to have been *ionized*).

When atoms join together to form molecules they often do so by sharing one or more electrons. This is called a *covalent bond* and it is what holds the water molecule together. Like charges repel each other and repulsion between those electrons in the oxygen atom that are not shared with hydrogen pushes the two hydrogen atoms into positions separated by an angle of about 105°, as shown in the box in figure 25. The effect of this is to leave a small negative electric charge on the oxygen side of the molecule and a small positive charge on the hydrogen side. The two charges balance, so the molecule as a whole has no charge, but it is slightly positive on one side and negative on the other. Molecules of this kind are called *polar* and experiment 20 in *A Chronology of Weather* shows how you can easily demonstrate the polarity of water for yourself.

Figure 25: *The structure of water.*

Polar molecules attract each other. In the case of water, a bond forms between the hydrogen end of one molecule and the oxygen end of the next, as figure 25 shows. It is called a *hydrogen bond* and is fairly weak, but it is what gives water the high surface tension that makes it form drops (see page 64) because molecules at the surface are securely bonded to those on either side and below. Mercury is the only substance that is liquid at room temperature and has a higher surface tension than water.

While it is a liquid, the molecules of water are joined into groups by hydrogen bonds. When any substance is heated it expands. So does water, but less than most liquids. Heating makes molecules absorb energy. This makes them move faster, so they take up more space, which is what causes the expansion. Water molecules also vibrate faster when they are heated, but within their groups the hydrogen bonds are like strings tethering them and restricting their expansion. Heat water enough, however, and the molecules vibrate so violently they break their hydrogen bonds and escape. Free of their bonds, they can leave the liquid altogether and enter the air. All exposed surfaces of liquid water lose molecules this way, but the warmer the water the faster they lose them.

Energy is needed to break the hydrogen bonds. When water is heated its temperature rises, but extra heat is required to break the hydrogen bonds and change liquid water into water vapor, a gas. This extra energy is absorbed by the molecules without changing the temperature of the water and the same amount of heat energy is released when the bonds form again. For pure water at 32° F, 600 calories of energy must be absorbed to change one gram (1 g = 0.035 oz) from liquid to gas (evaporation). It is called *latent heat* and the latent heat of water is higher than that of any other substance.

When water molecules absorb talent heat the temperature of the water does not increase. The latent heat they absorb is supplied by their surroundings, no heat is returned, and so the surroundings lose heat. In other words, evaporation cools the air. We benefit from this property of water when sweat evaporates from our skin, thereby cooling it.

Condensation converts water vapor, a gas, into liquid, where molecules are linked by hydrogen bonds. The formation of those bonds deprives the molecules of some of their energy, which is released as latent heat. The bond represents the energy holding molecules together, so the amount released when they form is precisely the same as the amount absorbed when they break.

This has a very important influence on the way clouds form in unstable air. Warm air rises, its water vapor condenses, and the release of the latent heat of condensation warms the air again, making it rise higher. More vapor condenses and the air goes on rising until it reaches a level at which its density is the same as that of the surrounding air. This forms heaped, cumulus clouds or, if the air is very unstable and moist enough, cumulonimbus storm clouds (see page 89).

Latent heat is also absorbed when ice melts and released when water freezes. In this case, hydrogen bonds exist in both the liquid and the solid, but as water freezes more bonds form. Because fewer bonds are involved, less latent heat is released than when water vapor condenses. The freezing of one gram of water releases 80 calories. That is why the air often feels a little warmer when ice is forming and the absorption of the same amount of latent heat to melt ice makes the temperature drop during the thaw.

Water can also change directly between the solid and gaseous phases (between ice and water vapor) without passing through a liquid phase. This is called *sublimation* and it also absorbs and releases latent heat. Not surprisingly, since the energy of latent heat is used in the making and breaking of hydrogen bonds, the amount of latent heat involved in sublimation is the sum of those required for condensation-evaporation and freezing-thawing. It is 680 calories for each gram.

In ice, hydrogen bonds pull the molecules into a very complex but ordered structure in which each molecule is connected to four

Figure 26: *Sublimation: what happens when sublimation occurs.*

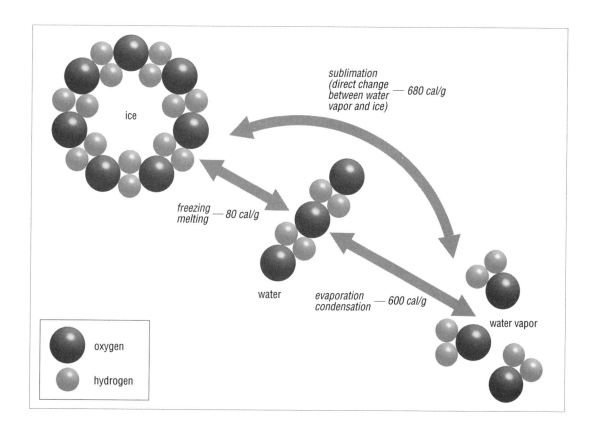

others. As figure 26 shows, the structure is fairly open. When the ice melts, some of the bonds break and the water molecules separate as groups once more. As groups, they can slide freely past one another and fill the spaces that existed in the crystal structure of the ice. The same number of molecules then occupy a smaller space, which is why water expands when it freezes, contracts when it thaws, and why it is at its most dense just above freezing, at 39° F. At sea-level pressure, at 50° F one cubic foot of pure water weighs 62.2 pounds, at 39° F it weighs 62.3 pounds, and as ice at 32° F it weighs only 57.1 pounds. As the temperature rises above 39° F ordinary expansion occurs. That is why ice floats, rather than sinking to the bottom.

We use water for washing and to dilute drinks, because many common substances will dissolve in it. Its solvent properties mean that natural water is never pure. Rain water carries substances dissolved into it while it was in the cloud and during its fall to the surface. Even over the middle of a large ocean, thousands of miles from the nearest land and even farther from any factory, rain contains carbon dioxide and sulfur dioxide dissolved from the air and it may also contain nitrogen oxides, produced when the energy of lightning oxidizes atmospheric nitrogen. Substances dissolve in water partly because of its polar molecules, which attract areas of opposite charge on their molecules. The presence of such impurities alters some of the properties of water, a fact we exploit when we scatter salt on roads to melt ice.

Salt is sodium chloride, NaCl, in which the bond (called an *ionic bond*) forms when a sodium atom donates one electron to a chlorine atom. This leaves the sodium atom short of one electron, giving it a positive charge (written as Na^+) and the chlorine atom with an extra electron (written as Cl^-) and it is the attraction of opposite charges which holds the molecule together. In water, the sodium and chlorine separate, the sodium being attracted to the oxygen end of a water molecule (O^-) and the chlorine to the hydrogen end (H^+). The sodium and chlorine are attached to and completely surrounded by water, but one consequence is that the freezing temperature is reduced. Water containing 25 parts of salt to 1,000 parts of water freezes at about 30° F. If the temperature is barely below freezing, the addition of salt will be enough to melt any ice forming on a road surface.

Snowflakes and types of snow

S now comes in many varities. Sometimes huge snowflakes drift slowly downwards, each one different from all the others. Catch one and you can admire its delicate beauty. At other times the flakes are small and hard. Examine them under a magnifying glass and they may look like tiny rods or needles, perhaps joined at their ends to make crosses or straight arms radiating from a central point. The possibilities are bewildering.

As a group of water molecules locks into the shape of an ice crystal it is affected by several forces. The most important of these are surface tension and the latent heat released by freezing. Surface tension pulls molecules toward one another and tends to smooth the surface. When you make ice cubes in a freezer, or when a pond freezes over, the surface of the ice is smooth. This is because it froze first at the surface, from the outside in. The latent heat escaped into the air and the sides of the container, leaving surface tension as the dominant physical force.

Snowflakes do not form in this way. They freeze onto a freezing nucleus, from the inside out, and the latent heat has to travel outward from the center before reaching the air. This tends to destabilize the crystal. Molecules are warmed enough to loosen their hydrogen bonds, so they move slightly away from the crystal surface, but are held by surface tension. Now projecting from the crystal, they are in a good position to gather fresh groups of molecules as the crystal falls. These groups freeze onto the projections and release their latent heat, surface tension and the destabilizing influence of diffusing latent heat working against one another. As the projection grows larger it sweeps more and more water molecules from the air through which it is traveling. The projections are the growing tips, like the growing tips of a plant. The bigger the flake grows, the more it is affected by the diffusion of latent heat and the less important surface tension becomes. Really large flakes form when smaller flakes touch and attach themselves together. By the time it reaches the ground, a snowflake may comprise 50 or more individual crystals clumped together.

Surface tension affects individual molecules and influences the shape of the first part of the crystal to form. With water molecules, the shape of the crystal is such that projections are most likely to develop in six directions. Most snowflakes, but by no means all, have six sides or six branches.

Once a projection from a crystal reaches a certain size, its edges become unstable and it starts producing smaller growing tips of its own. All around the flake the projections experience the same environment and the same forces act on them in the same way, so they respond in the same way. They all grow at more or less the same rate. This results in an almost perfectly symmetrical flake. It is the symmetry of its delicately branching form that makes a snowflake so beautiful. Frost on plants and window panes, grows in the same way, freezing from the inside out, and it also produces delicate, intricate patterns.

Each snowflake is symmetrical, but it is also different from all the other snowflakes around it. This is because each flake follows its own path as it falls. Snowflakes fall slowly through air that is moving. They may be caught in upcurrents or deflected to one side or the other. Some remain airborne longer than others. These movements carry them into regions where the temperature is a fraction of a degree higher or lower, there is a little more or less moisture, or a variation in the number and type of solid particles, which affects the rate at which water condenses and freezes. Each flake responds to the conditions it experiences, but no two flakes are exposed to quite the same conditions.

Big snowflakes fall when the temperature is fairly mild. If the temperature inside the cloud is between 32° F and 23° F, a very thin film of water coats the surface of each ice crystal. When two crystals touch, this film freezes, binding the crystals together. Air beneath a cloud is usually warmer than air inside it, so when they leave their cloud big flakes often fall through air that is barely below freezing and may be above it. If the air temperature is higher than about 30° F, the snow may reach the ground but then melts quickly. It will not settle.

Obviously, water must be present for ice crystals to form at all and the more water there is the larger the snowflakes are likely to be. The availability of moisture is also linked to temperature, because the warmer air is the more water vapor it can hold and the water molecules from which ice crystals are made must be carried by the air as vapor. Air at around freezing temperature can hold nearly six times more water vapor than air at 0° F. This is another reason big snowflakes form at mild temperatures. More moisture is available to them.

Snowflakes can grow big where the temperature is mild, but only if the cloud itself is tall enough for temperatures near the top to be much lower. At temperatures higher than about -40° F ice crystals will not form at all unless freezing nuclei are present and most freezing nuclei initiate the formation of crystals between 10° F and -13° F. If the temperature is higher than this throughout the cloud, any precipitation will fall as rain. If the raindrops are supercooled and the temperature beneath the cloud is below freezing, it will be freezing rain. When it snows with big, gentle flakes, you may be sure the temperature in the lower part of the cloud is only a little below freezing and that the cloud is tall, extending upward to a height where the air is very much colder.

What starts as a fall of big flakes may reach the ground as graupel, or soft hail. This tells you more about the cloud that produced it. Graupel is not true hail (see page 65), but a mixture of snow and ice. The process leading to it begins with the formation of ice crystals, at a very low temperature near the top of a tall cloud. As they fall, the crystals clump together into big flakes. This means the temperature is mild in the middle layers of the cloud and the air there is moist. At a still lower level the flakes encounter liquid droplets supercooled to just below freezing temperature, so the cloud is mixed, containing both ice crystals and water droplets. The droplets freeze onto the falling flakes, coating them with ice so they are like minute snowballs, and these are what reach the ground.

At really low temperatures the air can hold very little water vapor. When people say "it's too cold for snow," this is what they mean. Cold air is also dry air. Air dries as its water vapor condenses or crystallizes and the last of the vapor "squeezed" from the cooling air may form ice crystals. Like crystals in warmer air, they gather more water molecules as they fall, but moisture is already very scarce and they have few encounters. They grow slowly and at low temperatures they have no surface film of water that would allow them to clump, so they remain as tiny, compact splinters. If there is a wind to drive them, they are dense enough to sting when they hit your face. Examine them under a strong magnifying glass and you will see that some are like columns or needles and others have very irregular shapes.

The smallest ice crystals of all form at temperatures below about -20° F. These still require freezing nuclei, but when the temperature falls below -40° F water will freeze without nuclei. Such low temperatures are common at high altitudes. Near the tropopause, at about 33,000 feet over middle latitudes in winter, the temperature is about -70° F. Air this cold is too dry for there to be many ice crystals, but a little lower they are quite abundant in air that has been lifted along a weather front with colder, denser air. Despite being so far from the ground you can see them clearly. Indeed, they are a very common site as thin, wispy clouds of the cirrus type. Sometimes winds sweep them into long, thin strands, curled at the ends, called "mares' tails."

There are parts of the world where winter temperatures regularly fall below -20° F. They do so in polar regions, of course, but also in many parts of North America, Europe, and Asia. Occasionally relatively moist air may move into a very cold region and when this happens water may crystallize just as it does in cirrus-type clouds. In effect, these clouds form at low level and ice crystals will fall from them. Crystals also fall from high-altitude clouds, but sublime into vapor when they reach warmer air. Those which fall from low-level clouds may reach the ground before evaporating. They will fall as light snow composed of crystals the size of sugar grains.

After it has fallen, snow begins to change. Even in the coldest weather, bright sunshine often melts the topmost layer, which freezes again at night, so a thin crust of clear ice lies on top of the snow. Where the snow is deep a different type of change may take place at the base. Some of the crystals comprising the first snow-flakes to have fallen sublime and the resulting vapor immediately freezes again, but into much larger crystals, called *hoar*. This process then extends upward into the overlying snow. Hoar crystals are dense, but packed more loosely than the original snow and they flow readily. They weaken the snow and are a major cause of avalanches.

We use the single word *snow* to describe a number of distinct ways in which ice crystals form, grow, and subsequently change. This is because, despite the fact that many of us see at least some snow every winter, we are more familiar with liquid water, for which we have more names. We talk of "showers," "torrential rain," "cloudbursts," "drizzle," "mist," and "fog," all of which are types of liquid precipitation. Not surprisingly, people living in regions where water is frozen for most of the time have fewer words for types of rain and more for different types of snow.

Wilson Bentley, the man who photographed snowflakes

People have been fascinated by the beauty of snow and ice for thousands of years. In fact our word *crystal* is from the Greek word *krustallos*, which means ice.

This fascination was not confined to the west, of course, and although anyone examining snow closely might have realized that their crystals are hexagonal (six-sided) the first written record of this discovery is not European, but Chinese. It was made by Han Ying in a work called *Moral Discourses Illustrating the Han Text of the "Book of Songs,"* written some time between 140 and 131 B.C. From that time this fact about snowflakes was well known in China, but many centuries passed before any mention of it appeared in European writings.

Olaf Mansson, or to give him his Latinized name Olaus Magnus (1490–1557), the Archbishop of Sweden, is believed to have been the first. In 1555 he published a book on natural history in which he depicted snow crystals. A little later, in 1591, an English mathematician, Thomas Harriot (1560–1621), noted the same observation, but did not publish it. Johannes Kepler (1571–1630) also wrote a description of snowflakes, in *A New Year's Gift, or On the Six-cornered Snowflake*, published in 1611.

More detailed studies had to wait for the invention of the microscope. One of the early microscopists was the English physicist Robert Hooke (1635–1703). He became fascinated by the instrument, and improved it. His *Micrographia*, published in 1665,

contained his own detailed drawings of snowflakes and descriptions of their crystal structure.

In the following centuries, snowflakes were of interest mainly for their beauty. They inspired poetry and art, but their structure was of no great concern to scientists. This changed in 1931, when art and science combined in the work of Wilson W. Bentley.

Born in 1865, Wilson W. Bentley lived at Jericho, in northern Vermont. He was a farmer, but also a meteorologist and keen photographer. Snow is common in his part of the world and Bentley was fascinated by the beauty, symmetry, and endless variety of snowflakes. Each winter he spent many hours recording them, with

Figure 27: *Wilson Bentley photographing snowflakes.* (From *Snow Crystals*, Dover Publications, Inc., New York, 1931)

a microscope attached to his camera, eventually accumulating a collection of more than 5,000 pictures. He selected more than 2,000 of his photomicrographs (photographs taken through a microscope) and assembled them in a book, called *Snow Crystals*, which was published in 1931, the year he died.

His observations were so carefully made and his photographs of such high quality that they attracted the interest of scientists. Bentley was not quite alone. A Polish scientist, A. B. Dobrowolska, was also studying ice crystals and wrote many articles about them, but it was Bentley's pictures that really fired imaginations. Today you can still find copies of his book, and there are field guides to snow crystals. The classic scientific book on the subject by Ukichiro Nakaya, of the University of Hokkaido, Japan, who is a leading world authority on snow, also called *Snow Crystals*, was published in 1954.

Studying snowflakes is not easy. They are very fragile and easily damaged and, of course, they melt within seconds unless they are kept below 32° F. Shining a strong light on them in order to see them more clearly can be enough to destroy them. There is a solution to the problem, however. A weak solution of a polyvinyl plastic in a common solvent (ethylene dichloride) will capture snowflakes and other ice crystals. The solution is chilled to a degree or two below freezing and a thin coat of it painted onto a surface, such as glass or board, which has also been chilled. The coated plate is placed outdoors while it is snowing, left there until it has collected several snowflakes, then placed somewhere cold indoors for about 10 minutes while the solvent evaporates. After that it can be warmed gently to room temperature. The snowflakes melt, their water evaporates through the very thin plastic film covering them, and a perfect impression of them is left behind, permanently marking the plate. These snowflake impressions can be studied and photographed just as though they were the originals.

No two snowflakes are identical, but if you examine a large number of them you will find there are several distinct types. This has allowed scientists to work out a way of classifying them, and in 1951 an international system of classification was adopted for snowflakes, hailstones, and other forms of ice that falls as precipitation.

The classification divides ice crystals into ten types. *Plates* are six-sided flakes. *Stellars* are six-pointed flakes. *Columns* are rectangular crystals, sometimes joined together. *Capped columns* are like columns, but with a bar at each end; when two or more join together the bars remain. *Needles* are fine, splinter-like crystals, which may also be joined together. *Spatial dendrites* are crystals with many fine branches, like fern fronds, and you often see them as frost on window panes. *Irregular crystals* are clumped together chaotically, so they have no regular shape. The last three types are *graupel*, *sleet*, and *hail*. There is a symbol for each type (see figure 29) and

Figure 28: *A few of the 2,000 remarkable photographs of snowflakes taken by Wilson Bentley that were later assembled into the book* Snow Crystals.   (From *Snow Crystals*, Dover Publications, Inc., New York, 1931)

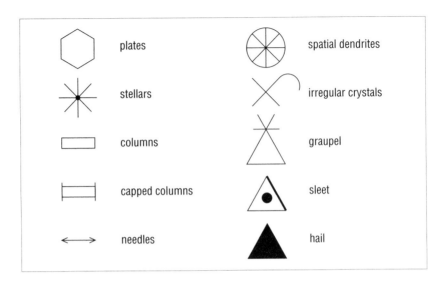

Figure 29: *Symbols for ice crystals.*

the types can be divided further into subtypes. A standard classification allows scientists to refer to ice crystals by names everyone understands.

Scientists now know a great deal about what happens when water freezes and how microscopically small crystals link together into big snowflakes. The stimulus for the research leading to these discoveries owes much to the magnificent photographs taken in the early years of this century by Wilson W. Bentley.

Cold air and warm water

At Brighton, on the south coast of England, there is a curious tradition. On New Year's Day, people bathe in the sea. Admittedly, they do not stay long in the water. For most a fast run into the sea and a fast run back to the beach is quite enough, but tradition holds that they must immerse themselves completely and duck their heads below the water, so they are wet all over. The event is usually filmed for the television news and shows the participants shivering and laughing. Unless they are good actors, they actually enjoy it.

Provided they remain in the water for only a very brief time, the ordeal may be less severe than it looks. Out of the water, the air temperature at Brighton on New Year's Day is, at best, only a degree or two above freezing and there is usually a wind to make it feel even colder (see page 103 for the effect of wind chill). The sea temperature on New Year's Day is usually around 50° F. During their run down the beach the bathers will feel very cold, but the water itself will feel distinctly warmer. Those who watch the event on television admire the courage of the bathers, or mock their silliness, on the basis of a false comparison. They know the coast in summer, when the air is warm and the sea feels very cold. In midsummer the sea is several degrees colder than the air over land, but in winter the situation is reversed.

Water must absorb much more heat than land before it becomes noticeably warmer and, once having absorbed heat, it is slower than land to lose it. In fact, it takes about five times more heat to warm water by a given amount than it takes to warm the same weight of dry sand. You need not live near the sea to check this for yourself. Experiment 21 in *A Chronology of Weather* shows you how to do it.

The amount of heat needed to warm a particular substance is known as the *heat capacity* of that substance and the heat capacity of water is much larger than that of any other common-place substance (see below).

The high heat capacity of water is another consequence of the hydrogen bonds linking its molecules (see page 72). What we feel as warmth on our skin is the energy with which molecules strike it. Warm a substance and its molecules move faster, so they strike our skin harder. Water molecules also move faster when they are warmed, but their hydrogen bonds restrict that movement. Much more heat energy is needed to accelerate them than would be needed if they were free to move independently of one another.

Heat capacity

The amount of heat required to raise the temperature of a unit mass of a substance by one kelvin (= 1° C) is known as the *heat capacity* (or specific heat capacity or thermal capacity) of that substance. In scientific units, the unit mass is one gram and the amount of heat is measured in joules (1 cal. = 4.186 J). This varies with temperature, so the temperature at which heat capacity is measured must always be stated.

The table below gives the heat capacity for a range of substances. In some cases the figures are averages.

Substance	Temp. (° F)	Heat capacity
dry air	68	1.006
ice	-6	2.0
ice	30	2.1
pure water	60	4.186
sea water	63	3.93
granite	68	0.80
granite	212	0.84
white marble	64	0.90
sand	68–212	0.80

Sea and land respond to solar radiation differently, and there is a further difference. Heat the surface of a substance and the heat is conducted beneath the surface. Eventually, the whole volume warms. How quickly it warms depends on its conductivity. Metals, for example, are good conductors of heat. Air is a very poor conductor and dry soil contains air between its particles, the amount varying according to the size of the particles. Sand is made from big particles and the spaces between them, called pores, are also big. Clay is made from very small particles and has less air-filled pore space. When the ground is heated by the Sun, the uppermost layer may warm quickly, but the temperature a foot or so below the surface may hardly change at all. If you have visited a sandy beach on a very hot day you will know that the sand can be too hot to walk on comfortably, but dig just below the surface and you reach cool sand. This variation of temperature with depth has been measured. On a hot, sunny day, the surface of the sand reached 104° F, but 2 inches below the surface the temperature was only 68° F, and at a depth of 6 inches it was 45° F.

Sand conducts heat poorly because of the amount of air it contains. At the same time as its temperature was being taken, so was the temperature of clay. At the surface the clay reached 70° F, cooler than the sand because heat was being conducted downward, away from the surface, much more efficiently through its small, closely spaced particles. At a depth of 2 inches the temperature was 57° F and at 6 inches 39° F.

If the soil is moist, however, heat is conducted deeper, because water is a better conductor of heat than air. So moist soil will absorb more heat than dry soil. If the soil is very moist it will absorb even more, because then the high heat capacity of water becomes important.

Not all the solar radiation that reaches the surface is absorbed. Some is reflected. How much is reflected varies from one surface to another and is measured as the albedo of that surface (see the table on page 44). Sand, for example, has an albedo of 35–45. That of water varies with the height of the Sun above the horizon. When the Sun is high, in the middle part of the day, water can have an albedo of about 2%, which means it absorbs 98% of the solar energy reaching it. Water is transparent, which means sunlight and heat penetrate below the surface. If the water is very clear, radiation can penetrate to about 30 feet. In fact the heat is usually carried much deeper, because water is seldom still. Waves and currents mix the water, carrying warm surface water far below the surface. In summer, the North Sea warms to a depth of about 130 feet.

These effects combine to magnify the different responses of land and sea to solar radiation. It is not simply that the sea warms and cools more slowly than the land, it does so much more slowly. This fact has major implications for our climates. In the first place, it allows us to distinguish distinct continental and maritime types of climate (see page 8). In winter, however, it can produce blizzards.

Picture what happens to a mass of air as it crosses a large continent. By late fall the land has lost the warmth it accumulated through the summer. It is cold and it chills the air passing over it. Cold air is also dry air, so by the time it reaches the far coast the air mass is cold and dry. Then it crosses the ocean. The water is warmer than the air, so the air warms a little. This increases its capacity to hold moisture and water evaporates into it. By the time it reaches the far side of the ocean it has become relatively mild, moist, maritime air. Now it encounters land again, and is chilled. As it moves inland, its temperature falling, it starts losing its moisture, and in winter it is likely to lose it in the form of snow, possibly driven by strong winds. In other words, there are blizzards.

It is not even necessary for the air to cross an ocean. Any large body of water can trigger blizzards in winter. The Great Lakes of North America often do so.

As fall advances the Great Lakes cool very slowly, remaining free of ice well into the winter. In some winters they do not freeze over at all. Air that crosses them is continental. It has traveled over cold land. As it crosses the lakes it warms and picks up moisture. Then it reaches the cold, continental land mass again. Its temperature falls rapidly, its water vapor condenses, and snow falls. Parts of northern Michigan have received around 33 feet of snow in a single winter and the average snowfall is more than 16 feet. At Hooker, New York, about 39 feet of snow fell in the winter of 1976–77. Snowfall is not spread evenly, of course, with so much falling every day to make up the total. Much of it arrives during storms, as blizzards. In December 1937, a storm dropped 4 feet of snow on Buffalo, New York, in a single day and by the time a five-day storm ended in January 1966, nearly 8.5 feet of snow had fallen on Oswego, New York.

Over the years, these places average much higher snowfalls than places in the same latitude but farther away from the Great Lakes. They lie in a "snowbelt" extending downwind for about 30 miles from the nearest lake shore. No other continent has a snowbelt comparable to that of North America because in no other continent is there a large enough area of water in the right location to produce one. Lake Baikal, in Siberia, is the eighth largest lake in the world and it influences the climate of the region around it, making it warmer in winter and cooler in summer, but in fall it causes fog rather than snow, and by the middle of December it has frozen completely.

Once the surface freezes over the supply of moisture is cut off and the snowbelt effect ends. Within the snowbelt it is possible to tell whether heavy snowfalls are likely. They depend on the surface remaining unfrozen and on the difference in temperature between the water and the air crossing it. The warmer the water and colder the air the more evaporation there will be, and if the air is very cold so will the surrounding land be, triggering rapid condensation and precipitation.

Were it not for the high heat capacity of water, there would be little difference in temperatures over land and sea and in high latitudes much of the sea would freeze over in winter. Its heat capacity is one more remarkable property of water. It gives maritime regions milder winters than they would have otherwise, but it also delivers fierce snowstorms.

Snowstorms, drifting, and blizzards

When someone says "Six inches of snow fell last night," what do they mean? We often talk about the amount of snow that falls as though this were a precise figure we could estimate simply by looking out of the window. Step outdoors, however, and you may or may not see 6 inches of snow. More probably you will find some places where the snow lies 3 inches deep, others where it is more than a foot deep. So how can we arrive at a figure of 6 inches?

Snow is not like rain. Being liquid, rain flows. On open ground, away from shelter, one inch of rain is the same everywhere. Snow does not flow. It accumulates where it lands and the wind carries it to particular places, so more accumulates in some places than in others. Nor is all snow the same. Wet snow, falling as big flakes, takes up more space than dry, powdery snow.

Perhaps, then, we should be more specific. When we talk of "six inches of snow," perhaps we should state what kind of snow we mean and where this 6-inch depth is to be found and whether it is typical.

There is really only one way to deal with the problem and that is to be careful in choosing where to measure the depth of snow and then to convert snowfall into its rainfall equivalent. This is what meteorologists do and the result tells them something more useful than the amount of snow. It tells them how much water fell. You can measure snowfall in the same way, as its rainfall equivalent. This is more complicated than measuring rainfall with a rain gauge, but the procedure is not difficult and experiment 22 in *A Chronology of Weather* explains how to do it.

One of the worst blizzards of modern times struck the area around Buffalo, New York, in late January 1977. Buffalo lies in the snowbelt east of the Great Lakes (see page 85) and several feet of snow fall in most winters, but the 1977 blizzard was much worse. Moist winds from Canada, blowing at 70 MPH for five days, deposited 4 feet of snow on top of the 3 feet that had fallen earlier in the winter. In places the drifts were 30 feet deep.

Drifting is caused by the wind. It is not the force of the wind that matters so much as the amount of snow it carries, although the two are sometimes related. If the wind is strong enough it will lift lying snow from the ground, adding it to the load that is falling. That is what happened at Buffalo. The gale picked up snow lying on the frozen surface of Lake Erie and drove it into the city.

Except on the open plains and over the sea, the wind near ground level rarely blows from the same direction for very long and both its direction and strength vary from place to place. Hills, trees, buildings, and obstructions of every kind deflect it and this effect is strongest in cities, especially cities where buildings are of different heights.

Obstructions and friction with the ground combine to slow the wind. Climb a few hundred feet above ground level and wind speeds usually increase, often by a large amount. So cities tend to be a little less windy than the countryside surrounding them. On one occasion, for example, when the wind speed at Heathrow Airport, on the western outskirts of London, was measured as 6.4 MPH the wind in central London was blowing at 4.7 MPH. That was in the middle of the day, however, and at night the situation reversed, with the wind blowing harder in the city center than on the outskirts.

This happens because the ground surface cools at night, but in a large city vehicles and buildings release a great deal of heat, especially in winter. This forms a "heat island." Warm air rises over the city and meets cooler air above. The resulting mixing makes the airflow turbulent and turbulence brings air from above the city down to street level. This air is still moving at its original speed, so the wind blowing far enough above the buildings not to be much slowed by them is brought to ground level. The stronger the wind, the greater is the difference between city and rural wind speeds.

This is a general effect and the details can vary. A long, straight, city street with tall buildings on either side is like a canyon. If a wind is blowing approximately parallel to the street the buildings can funnel the wind along, just as happens in a natural canyon. This accelerates the wind, because the same volume of air must travel the same distance in the same time, but along a constricted path.

Wind blowing in any direction other than parallel to the streets behaves in a much more complicated fashion. When the wind strikes the face of a building some of the flow is deflected upward and some downward. At roof level, air deflected upward meets the main flow again and rejoins it, but on the downwind (lee) face of the building air is being drawn away by the wind and the pressure is slightly reduced. This draws some air down the side of the building as an eddy. At ground level, some of the air deflected down the face of the building flows back into the street, where it may meet air approaching from the building across the street. Where the two airflows collide they often spiral around one another, forming a street-level vortex. When you see bits of paper and dust whirling in a circle, it is because they are caught in an eddy vortex of this kind. The rest of the air moving down the face of the building spills to the sides, forming more eddies.

Overall, the effect of all this obstruction and turbulence is to slow down the wind and the stronger the wind the more it is slowed by its passage through the city. This affects the way snow falls. If snow is carried by a wind blowing directly onto the face of a building, some of its snow will stick to the walls, but this is a minor effect. If the wind literally blew snow onto walls it would cover them with a thick, fairly even layer. Snow might then fall under its own weight, slithering down the wall the way it will slither off a sloping roof. That is not what happens, of course. The snow collects at the foot of the wall, but not because it has fallen down the side of the building. The foot of the wall is where it fell in the first place.

Slowing the wind reduces its energy and the amount of any material the wind can carry depends on how much energy it possesses. In this the wind is very like a river. A fast-flowing river carries silt, sand, and small stones. After heavy rain river water is often brown because of the large quantity of material it is carrying. As the river slows, its energy is reduced and the heavier particles, such as stones, sink to the bottom. It can no longer carry them and as its energy continues to fall more and more of its load sinks, the

Figure 30: *The city of Philadelphia digs out after a blizzard in January 1996.* (Courtesy of Chandra Speeth)

heaviest particles first. Similarly, as the wind loses energy it, too, starts to drop the load of material it has been carrying.

Snowdrifts will develop wherever the wind loses energy. It loses energy by being deflected when it strikes the face of a building. Predictably, therefore, it will drop some of its load of snow, which will fall at the base of the building. That is why snow tends to pile up against the sides of houses, so you may have to dig your way out of the door after a heavy overnight fall.

Roads can be blocked by snow. In effect, a drift fills the road, sometimes to the height of the land to either side so the road disappears. Tall poles often line roads in places prone to heavy snowfalls to help travelers and snowplow drivers locate the road. Where the road surface is at the same level as the ground to either side, the entire area may be covered evenly. Where the road runs low, below the level of the land on either side, wind eddies with little energy will drop more snow onto the road than falls elsewhere, forming a drift starting on the lee side of the road. Sunken roads are likely to be in shade most of the time, so when the thaw arrives their drifts can persist for weeks longer than snow on more exposed ground.

Blizzards, driven by fiercely strong winds, can produce deep drifts, but so can even the gentlest breeze. The less energy the wind has to start with, the more easily that energy may be diminished. In still air, snow falls vertically downwards and every surface exposed to it is covered equally. Drifts can form under these conditions, but they are uncommon. Usually there is some air movement and the snow falls at an angle to the vertical. Where it meets obstructions it loses the little energy it has and snow accumulates.

Drifts are a major inconvenience and clearing them from blocked roads can be a slow, costly operation. They are also extremely dangerous, because it is difficult, and in unfamiliar terrain impossible, to estimate their depth or even to see them and a person who falls into one may have great difficulty escaping. In February 1799 a woman called Elizabeth Woodcock was walking home from a market in Cambridge, England, to the village of Impington, a distance of 3 miles. She fell into a snowdrift and was trapped there for eight days. By the time rescuers arrived she had heard the nearby church bells ring twice. Fortunately she was still alive and made a full recovery. Not everyone is so lucky.

Heavy snowstorms and what causes them

Severe storms, of the kind that bring torrential rain in summer and heavy snow in winter, form in very unstable air. As well as rain or snow, they often produce hail, thunder and lightning, and

Air pressure, highs and lows

When air is warmed it expands and becomes less dense. When air is chilled it contracts and becomes more dense.

Air expands by pushing away the air around it. It rises because it is less dense than the air immediately above it. Denser air flows

Pressure gradient and wind speed.

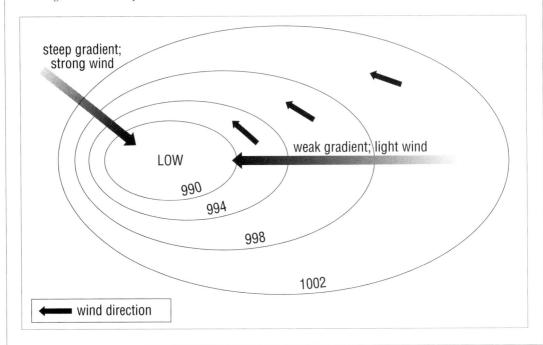

steep gradient; strong wind

LOW

990

994

998

1002

weak gradient; light wind

◀━━ wind direction

strong winds. In extreme cases they can trigger tornadoes, although these rarely happen in winter.

Near coasts, winter is a time of squalls, which are violent but isolated storms. They develop when skies are clear. At night, the land cools, radiating into the sky the warmth it absorbed during the day. If the sky is cloudy, the clouds absorb the heat radiated from below, warming the air and the ground beneath, so in winter clear nights are colder than cloudy nights. In winter the sea is warmer than the land (see page 82) and it continues to warm the air above it by night as well as by day. The result is that after a clear night very cold air will lie over the land and much warmer, moist air over the sea. If the warm air then moves over the coast it will rise above the cold air, become unstable, and that is what produces huge cumulonimbus storm clouds.

On a much larger scale, violent storms sometimes develop ahead of an advancing cold front (see box on page 14) along a "squall line" that may extend for hundreds of miles. There are several ways in to replace it, is warmed by contact with the surface, and also expands and rises. Imagine a column of air extending all the way from the surface to the top of the atmosphere. Warming from below causes expansion; as a result, surrounding air is pushed out of the column, so air remaining is less dense (contains fewer molecules of air) than it did when it was cooler. Because there is less air in the column, the pressure its weight exerts at the surface is reduced. The result is an area of low surface pressure, often called simply a *low*.

In chilled air the opposite happens. The air molecules move closer together, so the air contracts, becomes more dense, and sinks. The amount of air in the column increases, its weight increases, and the surface atmospheric pressure also increases. This produces an area of high pressure, or simply a *high*.

At sea level, the atmosphere exerts sufficient pressure to raise a column of mercury about 30 inches (760 mm) in a tube from which the air has been removed. Meteorologists call this pressure one *bar* and measure atmospheric pressure in *millibars* (1,000 millibar [mb] = 1 bar = 10^6 dynes cm^{-2} = 101,325 pascals).

Air pressure decreases with height because there is less air above to exert pressure. Pressure measured at different places on the surface is corrected to sea level pressure to remove differences due only to altitude. Lines are then drawn, linking places where the pressure is the same. These lines, called *isobars*, allow meteorologists to study the distribution of pressure.

Like water flowing downhill, air flows from high to low pressure. Its speed, which we feel as wind strength, depends on the difference in pressure between the two regions. This is called the *pressure gradient*. On a weather map it is calculated from the distance between isobars, just as the distance between contours on an ordinary map allows the steepness of hills to be measured. The steeper the gradient the stronger the wind.

Moving air experiences friction with the surface. This slows it more over land, where the friction is greater, than over the sea. Air is also subject to the Coriolis effect, which swings it to the right in the northern hemisphere and to the left in the southern hemisphere. As a consequence, winds do not cross the isobars at 90°. Over the oceans they cross at about 30° and over land at about 45°.

a squall line can occur. If the cold air behind the front is moving fast and sinking at the same time, it can push strongly beneath the warm air ahead of it. Alternatively, heavy rain may cool the air around it. That will make it sink and push under adjacent warmer air within the same air mass, where it is not raining, creating a false front. In addition, very large thunderstorms can "reproduce." An individual storm seldom lasts for more than an hour or two before it breaks down and dissipates, but if the rising and descending air inside the cloud divide into separate upcurrents and downcurrents, strong downcurrents, flowing out of the base of the cloud, may flow under adjacent air, pushing it upward and making it unstable.

Whatever the mechanism, all storms require an area of low pressure containing moist, unstable air (see box on pages 90–91) and a disturbance to set the unstable air in motion. Once these requirements are met, storm clouds will grow rapidly and the storm itself will follow.

Whether air is stable or unstable is a matter of *lapse rates.* Air temperature decreases with height. At the surface, the average temperature over the world as a whole is 59° F and at the tropopause, the boundary at about 36,000 feet above which temperature remains constant with further increases in height, averages are -74° F. Subtracting one temperature from the other shows that air temperature decreases by 133° F between sea level and 36,000 feet, or by 3.7° F for every 1,000 feet. This is the average lapse rate, but locally lapse rates vary widely. The actual local lapse rate is called the *environmental lapse rate.* In winter, for example, the surface temperature may be, say, 30° F, in which case the environmental lapse rate will be 2.9° F per 1,000 feet.

Suppose dry air is forced to rise, perhaps to cross a mountain. As it rises it will expand and cool at the dry adiabatic lapse rate (see box on page 4) of 5.5° F per 1,000 feet. This rate of cooling is constant, regardless of the initial temperature of the rising air. As it rises it cools faster than the average lapse rate. Imagine the surface air temperature is 30° F and the rising air starts at 31° F. By the time it reaches 1,000 feet, the temperature of the rising air will be 25.5° F and that of the surrounding air 27.1° F. The rising air is cooler, and therefore denser, than the air around it, so as soon as it has cleared the mountaintop it will sink and warm adiabatically until it reaches air at its own temperature. This air is said to be stable.

If the rising air is moist, however, it may soon cool to its dew-point temperature, at which water vapor starts to condense. Condensation releases latent heat, warming the air, and so further cooling will be at the saturated adiabatic lapse rate of about 3° F per 1,000 feet. The height at which condensation starts is called the lifting condensation level. Imagine it is at 200 feet, where the rising air will have cooled from 31° F to 29.9° F. Its rate of cooling then slows and at 1,000 feet its temperature is 27.8° F. This is warmer than the surrounding air at 27.1° F, so it will go on rising. Air that continues to rise is said to be unstable.

Now see what happens when the difference in starting temperatures is greater. If the rising air starts at 40° F and reaches its lifting condensation level at 500 feet and continues to cool at the saturated adiabatic lapse rate it will still be warmer than the surrounding air at 30,000 feet. It will rise all the way to and then through the tropopause, because it will still be warmer than air in the lower stratosphere. Such air would be very unstable indeed and would certainly produce huge storms, although air is not often as unstable as this. It reaches a height at which it has lost so much of its moisture that condensation ceases and its further cooling is at the higher dry adiabatic lapse rate.

Inside the cloud, conditions are very violent. Its base is at the lifting condensation level of 500 feet. Minute water droplets are carried upward in the rising air. Above about 14,000 feet, where the temperature is around -3° F, the droplets freeze into ice crystals, but continue to rise. Cold air sinks from the top of the cloud, so there are upcurrents and downcurrents with speeds that often reach 20 MPH and can exceed 60 MPH, but the most violent storms occur when wind above the cloud carries away the rising air. This draws more air from below and intensifies the upcurrents. Rising air swept away from the top of the cloud often forms a distinctive anvil shape, visible because of the ice crystals in it. If you see a big, dark cloud with a white anvil at the top, you can expect a violent storm.

At the center of a storm the air pressure is low, sometimes very low. Air drawn into the low will spiral around it, generating winds with speeds proportional to the pressure gradient (see page 59). Rain falling from the cloud will be driven by a strong wind, with even stronger gusts ahead of it, where air is being drawn into the upcurrents, and behind, where the cold downcurrents flow out of the cloud. If the precipitation falls as snow, blizzards are very likely.

Water droplets and ice crystals are rising, ice crystals are descending, and there are many collisions. Graupel and hailstones grow in this mixture of water and ice, and so do snowflakes (see page 74).

Something else also happens. Some of the particles acquire a slight surplus of oxygen and others a slight surplus of hydrogen. It occurs because hydrogen atoms can easily be made to separate from water molecules. Indeed, although the chemical formula for water is usually written as H_2O it can also be written as H–OH. For reasons that scientists still do not fully understand, the bursting of graupel pellets and splintering of colliding hailstones leaves a surplus of hydrogen on the smallest ice crystals and an oxygen surplus on the larger ice fragments and liquid droplets. Being lighter, the smallest particles accumulate at the top of the cloud and the largest at the bottom and so the water in the cloud separates. Hydrogen carries a positive electric charge, an oxygen atom bonded to one hydrogen atom (OH, called hydroxyl) carries a negative charge, and so the top of the cloud becomes electrically positive and the bottom negative.

Air is a good insulator, but eventually the electrical field produced by this charge separation can amount to more than 300,000 volts per foot and the insulation is overcome. The result is a spark of lightning. If it flashes inside the cloud or between one cloud and another we see it as an overall white light, called *sheet lightning*. *Forked lightning* is a spark between the negative base of the cloud and a local area of positive charge on the ground, traveling along an irregular path where the air offers least resistance. Before it reaches the ground, the first flash, called the stepped leader, causes a return flash. It travels upward along the same path and it is the flash we see.

A lightning flash rarely lasts longer than about 0.2 second, but in this time so much energy is released that the air through which the spark travels is heated to an extreme temperature and expands so fast it explodes, sending out the shock waves we hear as thunder. These travel at the speed of sound, which is much slower than the speed of light, so if the storm is some distance away we see the lightning before we hear the thunder. At a distance of one mile, we see the lightning approximately 2 seconds before we hear the thunder.

Thunder often keeps on rumbling for several seconds. This is because a lightning flash extends between the lower part of the cloud and the ground, a distance of half a mile or more, producing thunder along its whole length. Sound reaches us first from the nearest part of the flash, with more sound following from more distant parts. The rumbling of thunder has nothing at all to do with echoes from hills or buildings.

Beneath such a fearsome cloud precipitation is certain and it will be heavy. In the upper part of the cloud most of the water is frozen and ice crystals will clump together into snowflakes. Whether these survive all the way to the ground depends on the temperatures they experience as they fall. The lower the freezing level, which is the height at which the temperature falls to 32° F, the more likely it is to fall as snow and snow is unlikely if the freezing level is above 1,000 feet.

In our imagined cloud the freezing level is just above 2,000 feet, so it seems snowflakes and ice crystals have a long way to fall through air at higher than freezing temperatures. If the freezing level is to be at 1,000 feet and the lifting condensation level at 500 feet,

Figure 31: *Storm development up a slope.*

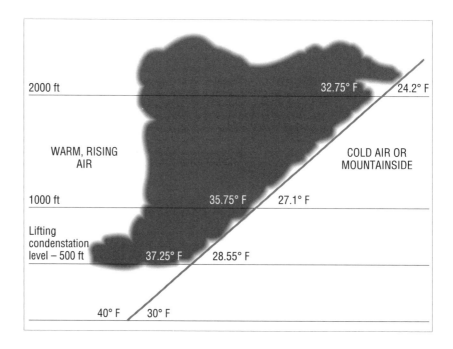

the surface temperature of the air must be 36.25° F, rather than our supposed 40° F.

It sounds as though this cloud will deliver rain, but perhaps not. Passage over mountains (called *orographic lifting*) is only one mechanism that can force air to rise. Cold air undercutting warmer air at a front will also cause lifting and can trigger instability in the same way. In fact, this is how most storms begin.

The warm air starts with a surface temperature of 40° F. The base of the cloud, at 500 feet, is at 37.25° F and at 1,000 feet the temperature is 35.75° F. Snow and ice will not melt very rapidly at these temperatures. Remember, though, that the air has been forced to rise up the slope of a mountainside or front. Cloud starts to form at 500 feet, where the air is cold enough for water vapor to condense, but the visible cloud base follows the slope, as figure 31 shows. Precipitation does not follow the slope, of course. It falls vertically (and is then driven by the wind). If it is a mountainside that forms the slope that is where the precipitation will fall. If the slope is frontal, precipitation will fall through the frontal zone into the air beneath.

Even at 500 feet, where the temperature inside the cloud is 37.25° F, that in the cold air beside it is 28.55° F. Precipitation falling from any higher level in the cloud will pass out of the cloud at a temperature barely above freezing and into much colder air extending all the way to the ground. Consequently it will fall as snow.

Snow will not fall if it forms above about 1,000 feet and the air below it is warm. Even in the middle of summer, the clouds that produce showers and storms in middle latitudes are full of snow, but it all melts before reaching the ground and falls as rain. Obviously, the air must be cold before snow will fall. Less obviously, the air producing the snow must be relatively warm.

Cold waves

Over most of Europe, from Britain as far south as northern Italy, January 1987 brought a spell of bitterly cold weather. In some places temperatures were the lowest of the century. Icy winds from Siberia blew across the continent and there were heavy snowfalls.

While Europeans shivered, Americans were enjoying an unusually mild winter. It lasted until April, but then the weather turned very cold in the central and southern states. Winds from the north, called *northers*, brought a blast of cold air down the eastern side of the Rockies, all the way from the Canadian Arctic. This was uncomfortable, but it brought a blessing. The low temperatures prevented development of the conditions that generate tornadoes.

Ordinarily, there are more than 100 tornadoes in April, the month when they are most likely, but in April 1987 only 20 were recorded. As a result, there were fewer tornadoes in 1987 than there are in most years.

Mongolia and China also experience spells of weather much like the northers of the United States. Behind depressions (areas of low pressure) that cross from west to east, cold air is drawn from the north and temperatures plummet.

These spells of very cold weather are called *cold waves*. They arrive suddenly and the temperature falls rapidly. In the northern, northeastern, and central parts of the United States a cold wave is defined as a fall in temperature of at least 20° F to no higher than 0° F within 24 hours. In California, Florida, and the Gulf Coast states, the temperature must fall by 16° to no more than 32° F within 24 hours. "Cold wave" is not defined so precisely elsewhere in the world, but the phenomenon is not confined to North America. It happens throughout the middle latitudes and can have a variety of causes.

Such rapid falls in temperature are extremely disruptive. Roads are blocked with snow, rail tracks are coated with ice and points freeze solid, plumbing freezes, and telephone and power lines break under the weight of snow or ice. Transport and communications systems fail and businesses have to close.

They are also dangerous. The 1987 European cold wave claimed nearly 300 lives, each year they kill more than 350 people in the United States, and these are only the deaths directly attributable to the weather. Sudden extreme cold can accelerate the deaths of people who are already weakened by old age or sickness. In Britain, it was estimated that the death rate increased by about 2,000 during the 1987 cold wave. It is not only humans who suffer. Sheep suffer greatly, and severe cold spells sometimes coincide with the start of the lambing season. Wild animals may starve because their food is frozen or deeply buried. In 1963, a cold wave in Britain killed huge numbers of wild birds.

Cold waves have occurred throughout history. They affect only the middle latitudes and they have nothing to do with long-term climatic trends. Whether the global climate is warming or cooling, cold waves can still erupt to bring misery. It is as though the Arctic winter invades and that is pretty much what happens.

Middle latitudes are where polar and tropical air meet as part of the global circulation of the atmosphere (see box on page 6). At the equator, warm air rises, cools, and loses most of its moisture from clouds that sometimes reach to 60,000 feet. That is why equatorial climates are wet. At high altitude, the air moves away from the equator, to north and south. Now extremely cold and dense, it sinks into the subtropics, warming adiabatically as it descends. Because it lost its moisture over the tropics, it is very dry and produces a belt of desert climates in both hemispheres. Some of this air flows back toward the equator at low level and some flows away from the equator. High over the poles, the air is extremely cold and dense. It sinks and flows away from the poles at low level. At around latitude 50°, cold air flowing away from the poles meets warm air flowing away from the equator. The converging air rises and at a high level some flows toward the poles and some toward the equator.

Where the polar and tropical air meet, a boundary, called the *polar front*, separates them, extending all the way to the tropopause, at about 40,000 feet. Because the tropical air is warmer and less dense than the polar air, it extends higher and the tropopause folds over, with warm air lying above cold air. It is at the tropopause that the difference in temperature between the two types of air is most marked. This difference generates a wind blowing at all levels up the slope of the front and reaching its maximum force at the top. Because it results from the difference in temperature it is called a *thermal wind* and thermal winds blow parallel to the front, in the northern hemisphere with the colder air to the left, from west to east. This high-level westerly wind is called the *polar front jet stream*. It forms a narrow band, between 30,000 and 50,000 feet, blowing at up to 150 MPH, but occasionally at 300 MPH in winter, when the temperature difference is greatest.

The jet stream drives the generally westerly movement of air in middle latitudes, but its strength and location vary. In summer, when high latitudes become warmer, the temperature difference between polar and tropical air is reduced. The westerly circulation weakens and the polar front jet stream moves toward the poles, crossing North America at about the latitude of the Great Lakes and Europe at about the latitude of Spain. In winter the jet stream moves farther toward the equator. It crosses North America from Mexico to North Carolina and on the other side of the Atlantic it crosses to the south of the Mediterranean.

These are average positions, however, and the polar front jet stream is highly variable. In spring and fall it is on the move between its summer and winter locations and, especially in late winter, it tends to break down completely over cycles lasting from 3 to 8 weeks. The cycle begins as a series of undulations in the direction of the jet stream. These grow bigger, until in some places the wind blows from the north, in other places from the south, although the overall air flow is still from west to east. After that the westerly flow breaks up into cells, where the flow is circular. Then the jet stream ceases altogether before establishing itself once more. This breakdown usually moves from east to west.

Weather systems in middle latitudes usually move from west to east with depressions following the line of the high-level, westerly jet stream. As the pattern changes, and the jet stream flows across lines of latitude rather than approximately parallel to them, the movement of air and weather systems at lower levels changes with it. This means there are places where air is being drawn from far to the north.

The jet stream flows parallel to the polar front, so in the northern hemisphere polar air lies to the north and tropical air to the south. As the front moves south in the fall, polar air extends to cover the area to its north. The depressions moving beneath the jet stream bring warmer air, however, and they can be extensive. They moderate temperatures, although continental climates, far from the warming effects of the oceans, always bring much colder winters than maritime climates.

Undulations in the jet stream are followed by the air behind the polar front. As it curves, tropical air moves north behind the *crests* of its waves, and polar air moves south behind the *troughs.* Some regions enjoy mild weather, brought by the northward migration of tropical air, but others are covered by polar air. This can extend far to the south, and cold waves due to the sudden incursion of polar air occasionally happen even in Alabama and Florida. Indeed, they are especially dangerous there, because people are used to a subtropical climate and are not expecting them. In 1965, a cold wave in these two states caused many deaths.

When the jet stream breaks down, the movement of weather systems ceases and then, too, cold waves can invade. The breakdown isolates large masses of air, which then remain stationary. In high latitudes these isolated masses often comprise dense air at relatively high atmospheric pressure (called *anticyclones*) and in winter this is cold, polar air. As the westerly movement of low-pressure areas resumes, the highs block their path, diverting them to north or south, and this blocking sometimes persists for weeks. From January to early March 1963, for example, the whole of the British Isles lay beneath a blocking anticyclone. Anticyclones bring fine weather, so skies are clear. This produces cold nights as there is no blanket of cloud to trap heat radiating from the ground. Further south, blocking is more commonly due to stationary depressions, which bring wet but fairly mild weather.

It is not the general weather associated with a winter anticyclone that brings a cold wave, however, but the air flow around the anticyclone. In the northern hemisphere, air moves in a clockwise direction around anticyclones. On the eastern side of a stationary anticyclone, the clockwise circulation draws air from far to the north. Over North America, this is cold, polar air from northern Canada. In western Europe, blocking anticyclones usually occur well to the north, exposing most of the region to easterly winds along the southern side of the high-pressure center. Easterly winds draw in bitterly cold air from central Asia.

Blocking anticyclones also occur in summer, of course. Then they bring prolonged periods of fine, warm, dry weather. In some places they cause droughts.

Ice storms

Early airplanes flew at low altitudes and only in fine weather. It was not until they were equipped with flight instruments that pilots began to venture through clouds rather than around or beneath them. Once that became possible, "instrument flying" was introduced into the training of professional pilots, who were required to take off, fly predetermined courses, and perform specified maneuvers with the windows of the airplane covered by opaque material.

Flight instruments inform the pilot of the attitude, height, speed, and direction of the aircraft. They were a major advance that allowed planes to fly in poor weather. While this improvement was being developed, new airframe and engine designs were making it possible for planes to fly at higher altitudes.

It was not long before a problem emerged. As planes flew through some clouds, but not all, ice would form on the wings and tail. Unless something was done to remove it, the ice could quickly grow into a layer thick enough to affect the airflow over the wings and control surfaces. Severely iced wings would no longer provide enough lift to keep the plane airborne and ice would jam the controls. Icing caused many crashes before aircraft were fitted with "de-icing boots," which were inflatable rubber pads along the leading edges of the wings and tail that expanded and contracted to break up the ice as it formed. Modern planes are equipped with heaters to melt ice. Pilots of planes lacking de-icing equipment learned to identify and avoid the types of cloud that were likely to cause icing.

Everyone had supposed that when water droplets cool to around 32° F they freeze. Ice crystals and snowflakes present no hazard to an aircraft because they do not stick to its smooth surfaces. In fact, of course, cloud droplets must be cooled to well below freezing temperature before they turn into ice. Supercooled droplets are common and they are what cause icing. When they collide with a surface they freeze onto it instantly, attaching themselves firmly to it, and a plane flying through a supercooled cloud sweeps up the droplets in its path.

Aircraft icing was dramatic and at first unexpected, but a very similar kind of icing has always been familiar at ground level. Trees can be covered in a thick coating of ice, radio masts can accumulate

Figure 32: *Icicles fringe the eaves of a house.* (Courtesy of Chandra Speeth)

huge masses of ice, usually on just one side, and overhead power and telephone lines can be enclosed in ice several times their own thickness. These are ice storms.

They are most likely to occur just ahead of a warm front, as illustrated in figure 33. Ahead of the front, in the cold air, the temperature is well below freezing, say 29° F, and objects in the cold air are at the same temperature. Behind the front, the warm air is just above freezing, say at 34° F, and this will be the temperature of the rain falling from the frontal cloud. The rain falls through the front and into the cold air. As it falls, the air cools it a little, so by the time it strikes the surface, or an object projecting from the surface, it is just about at freezing temperature.

To produce an ice storm, the rain must be heavy and driven by wind so it falls at an angle to the vertical. Then it will be driven against surfaces, such as the mast shown in the diagram, which are several degrees colder than freezing. As each raindrop strikes, the part of it touching the surface freezes instantly. The remainder spills to the sides and also freezes on contact. Before long, the exposed object is covered in ice.

If you walk, or even more if you ride a bicycle or motorbike through this kind of rain, you, too, will ice up. A layer of ice will form all over the front of your coat. It will not grow very thick, of course, because your own movement will constantly shatter the ice and make it fall off, but if you were to sit or stand still, you could find yourself encased.

The result is striking to look at. Radio masts are always located in exposed areas, on high ground, and they can accumulate an ice

Figure 33: *Ice storms.*

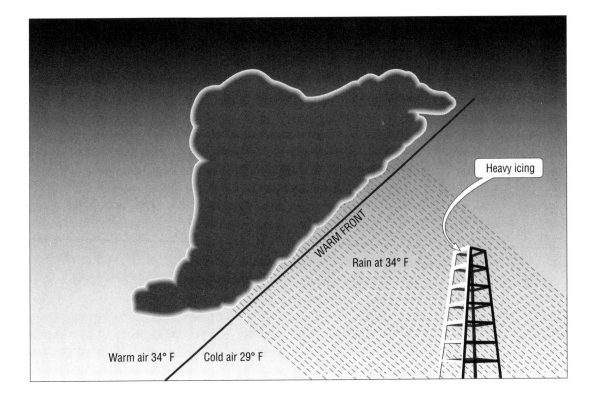

Warm air 34° F   Cold air 29° F

Figure 34: *Rime ice is made up of supercooled fog droplets that freeze as they strike cold objects. These feathers of ice grow into the wind, often to a length of two feet or more.* (Courtesy of the Mount Washington Observatory)

coating a foot or more thick. Ships at sea accumulate similar layers on their masts and rigging.

An ice storm produces a romantic winter scene, but it causes a great deal of damage. Ice is heavy. After a severe ice storm in southern England in January 1940, snapped telephone wires were found to be loaded with up to 1,000 pounds of ice and some of the poles broke when their load reached 11 tons of ice. Ice storms disrupt power supplies and communications and it can be days before services are restored. Branches, weighted with ice, fall from trees.

The effects on wildlife are even worse. Roosting birds have been known to freeze onto their branches, where they died from starvation, and ground-dwelling birds have remained grounded when their wings were coated with ice. Cats out on their nighttime prowls have also been stuck when their paws froze to the ground.

Wind chill, frostbite, hypothermia, and snow chill

Step outdoors on a windy day in winter and the wind feels cold. Even if you know the temperature has not fallen, the wind will make the air feel colder than it did before the wind started and if you move out of the wind, into a sheltered place, it will feel warmer. You are experiencing *wind chill* and at low temperatures this can be very dangerous.

Weather forecasts often mention the "wind chill factor" as a temperature lower than the predicted air temperature. Obviously, since wind is simply moving air and air cannot be colder than itself, this use of temperatures can be confusing. Forecasters report wind chill as a temperature because degrees are more familiar units than those they are really using, which are calories or joules per square inch or centimeter per second.

Our bodies maintain a constant internal temperature and if this varies outside fairly narrow margins we are ill. The internal heat is generated by the oxidation of the carbon in our food, and we use this energy to move and operate our bodies. We also lose heat from the surface of our skin and by breathing. When we breathe we inhale cold air, which is then warmed to body temperature in our lungs. This tends to cool the lungs and as the air warms, moisture evaporates into it, causing further cooling through the absorption of latent heat. Maintaining our constant body temperature depends on striking a balance between the rate at which we generate heat and the rate at which we lose it.

Clothing keeps us warm by reducing the rate at which we lose heat through the skin. It achieves this by trapping air in millions of tiny spaces. Heat from the skin warms this air, but the air can escape only slowly through the layers of our clothes. Wear too many clothes and we grow uncomfortably hot.

We are not usually fully covered by clothes, however, even when outdoors in winter. Our faces are likely to be bare and we do not always wear gloves. The face and hands can amount to as much as 10% of the total surface area of a human body. Bare legs can increase this to around 30%, but even bare skin is covered by a layer of warm air, just a few molecules thick, so on a calm day we still have some protection against heat loss.

That is where the wind attacks. It sweeps away this thin layer of warmed air. Our bodies respond by generating more heat in an attempt to replace it, but if it proves impossible to generate heat fast enough, the skin will grow colder and that is what we feel.

Just how cold the wind makes us depends on the air temperature and the wind speed. The wind chill factor can then be calculated quite precisely. With an air temperature of 40° F and a wind blowing at 10 MPH, for example, a body loses heat at the same rate as if the air temperature were 28° F and the air calm. Provided you are wearing adequate winter clothes this will not harm you, but at lower temperatures it can become serious.

Without going outdoors, it is not difficult to demonstrate the way wind accelerates cooling. Experiment 23 in *A Chronology of Weather* describes a simple method for doing this.

Wind chill increases rapidly as the temperature drops and the wind speed rises, although the effect tapers off as winds reach about 40 MPH. If the wind blows harder than this it will produce some additional wind chill cooling, but not much. Figure 35 is a table illustrating the effect. If you go outdoors when the thermometer reads 0° F while a 15-MPH wind is blowing, it will feel as though the temperature is -31° F, because your skin is cooling as fast as it would in calm air at that temperature.

At any temperature below about -21° F you need to be very well wrapped up, with no bare skin exposed, and if you start to feel the chill you should do something about it, because it can be dangerous. The conditions of wind and calm-air temperature producing this much wind chill are bordered by a thicker line on the chart. If the temperature effectively falls below about -71° F, conditions are dangerous. This is extreme cold and it can kill in a surprisingly short time. Winds and temperatures producing a dangerous amount of wind chill are bordered on the chart by the very thick line.

Figure 35: *Wind chill effect.*

Wind chill temperature (°F)

Wind speed (mph)	35	30	25	20	15	10	5	0	-5	-10	-15	-20	-25	-30	-35	-40
0	35	30	25	20	15	10	5	0	-5	-10	-15	-20	-25	-30	-35	-40
5	32	27	22	16	11	6	0	-5	-10	-15	-21	-26	-31	-36	-42	-47
10	22	16	10	3	-3	-9	-15	-22	-27	-34	-40	-46	-52	-58	-64	-71
15	16	9	2	-5	-12	-18	-25	-31	-38	-45	-51	-58	-65	-72	-78	-85
20	12	4	-3	-10	-17	-24	-31	-39	-46	-53	-60	-67	-74	-81	-88	-95
25	8	1	-7	-15	-22	-29	-36	-44	-51	-59	-66	-74	-81	-88	-96	-103
30	6	-2	-10	-18	-25	-33	-41	-49	-56	-64	-71	-79	-86	-93	-101	-109
35	4	-4	-12	-20	-27	-35	-43	-52	-58	-67	-74	-82	-89	-97	-105	-113
40	3	-5	-13	-21	-29	-37	-45	-53	-60	-69	-76	-84	-92	-100	-107	-115

Using the chart is straightforward, but you need to make some allowance for the wind speed quoted in weather forecasts. Close to the ground the wind is slowed by friction, especially in towns. To measure wind speed accurately and in a standard way, meteorologists mount their anemometers (instruments that measure wind speed) 33 feet above ground level. The wind there is stronger than it is at ground level, so you can expect to experience a wind no more than about two-thirds the strength given in the weather forecast, unless the forecaster specifies that it is ground-level wind speeds that are being quoted.

You should also remember that although the air may be calm, you will feel a wind if you move about in it. If you ride a bicycle at 15 MPH, a 15-MPH wind will blow on your face even on a windless day. If you walk briskly you will feel a wind of about 5 MPH. So a calm day is truly calm only if you stand still.

Intense cold causes injury in two ways. The first, but less dangerous, is frostbite. It is less dangerous because it is easily noticed and treated.

If you go out alone in intensely cold weather, always carry a small hand mirror in your pocket. From time to time, look at your face in the mirror. If you are with a friend, keep looking at one another. If you see a white patch, usually on the tip of a nose or an earlobe, that is the beginning of frostbite and you must do something about it. All bodily extremeties are at risk and if you stay in the cold for long you should also check your fingertips and toes. It is not a good idea to remove your boots and socks in subzero temperatures, but see if you have feeling in your toes. Can you wiggle them and feel them wiggling? There is no feeling in frostbitten tissue, so your toes are safe so long as you can feel they are still there.

Frostbite occurs because heat is carried away from exposed extremeties faster than it is from tissues better supplied with blood vessels. Blood has been withdrawn from the affected part, which is why it looks white, and cells within it are starting to freeze. This kills them, because as water inside the cells freezes it expands (see page 70), bursting their walls. You will feel nothing, because the nerve endings have also lost their blood supply.

Rubbing frostbite makes matters worse. It will simply increase the damage to already injured tissue without restoring the blood supply. Instead, the affected parts must be warmed slowly and gently. Bathing them gently in cold water is usually enough to thaw them, but then the victim should see a doctor.

Hypothermia is more dangerous. It develops slowly, with few early warning signs, and it can kill. *Hypo-* is from the Greek *hupo*, meaning "under," and as the name suggests hypothermia simply means "low temperature." The victim has lost so much body heat through the skin that the internal, or "core" temperature has fallen.

If it falls from the normal 98° F to 90° F the body can no longer restore it by its own efforts, and if it falls below 80° F there is a serious risk of death.

The first you may notice is that the victim starts talking nonsense and seems confused and forgetful. Speech may be slurred and vision impaired. The skin will feel very cold and the face and hands may look blue. If you are out walking, the patient may complain of tiredness or even grow drowsy, and may start shivering uncontrollably. This is an added danger. Ordinarily, shivering serves to warm us, because the rapid movement of muscles speeds up the metabolism and the rate at which blood is pumped to surface tissues. In hypothermia, however, the blood reaching the skin is chilled, returns into the body cold, and accelerates the fall in core temperature. Check the patient's pulse. Hypothermia victims have a weak pulse. If you can, take the patient's temperature. If this is below 95° F you must take immediate action.

On no account try to warm the hands and feet. This can send cold blood to the heart, leading to heart failure. Warm the center of the body first, with your own body if necessary. Remove wet clothing and wrap the patient in whatever dry clothing or blankets you can find. Allow the patient to rest and recover slowly. If you have any warm soup, encourage the patient to take some, but the soup must be warm, not hot, and the patient should not be given any hot drink or food. On no account give the patient alcohol.

Meanwhile, call an ambulance or the rescue services. Hypothermia is a medical emergency requiring professional treatment. If someone is suffering from both frostbite and hypothermia, deal with the hypothermia first.

Even when temperatures are well above freezing, wind chill can lead to hypothermia if people are exposed for a long time without moving and especially if their clothing is wet. Once your clothes are sodden the air spaces within them are filled with water and water is a much better conductor of heat than air. As you know, when you are caught in heavy rain without a coat you soon feel cold, even in summer.

This is the danger of snow. Being buried in snow can protect you from the wind and people caught outdoors in a blizzard can often survive by digging an ice cave and sheltering inside it. Once the snow starts to melt, however, you are at risk, because the latent heat needed to turn ice crystals into liquid water will be taken from your body. It is you who are melting the snow, and at the same time it is making you colder. This is snow chill. To make matters worse, when the snow has melted your clothes will be soaked in water only slightly above freezing.

Whiteout

A blizzard can render all our senses useless. That is why blizzards are so dangerous. Technically, a blizzard is defined as a snowstorm with winds of at least 35 MPH, a temperature no higher than 20° F, and visibility reduced to no more than one-quarter of a mile. As you will see from the wind chill chart on page 104, with a wind of 35 MPH an air temperature of 20° F will chill a human body as effectively as calm air at -20° F.

That is very cold, but if you are caught outdoors in this kind of weather at least you may be able to find your way to shelter. Visibility is reduced, but there is a good chance that you will still be able to see far enough to avoid being hopelessly lost. This is a mild blizzard, however, and blizzards can be much more severe. In a severe blizzard, the wind is at least 45 MPH, the temperature no higher than 10° F, and visibility is close to zero. You cannot see farther than a few feet and the effect of wind chill is to cool your body at a temperature equivalent to about -38° F.

We see the world around us because our eyes are sensitive to light reflected from objects and most of us rely mainly on our vision to orient ourselves. Plunged suddenly into darkness we are helpless. A blizzard does not produce darkness. If it occurs during daytime the daylight remains, but it is scattered.

The light will already be diffuse. If the blizzard includes falling snow, the sky will be cloudy and light passing through it will be scattered by ice crystals or water droplets in the clouds, making the entire sky a uniform white or gray. Without the airborne snow, objects would reflect this diffused light. They would be clearly visible, but would cast no shadows because light was shining on them evenly from all sides. The airborne snowflakes also reflect light and because they are twisting and turning as they move they reflect it in all directions. Then it is not only the sky above that is a uniform color and featureless, so is the air between the cloud and ground.

In these conditions a flashlight or car headlights are useless, just as they are in dense fog. When you shine a beam of light ahead of you it, too, is scattered by the droplets or snowflakes. It reveals nothing. Indeed, so much of it may be reflected directly back at you that it dazzles you, actually making the situation worse rather than better.

Fog at least allows you to see the ground beneath your feet, but a blizzard may make even this impossible. The air is white with snow, but so is the snow-covered ground. It becomes impossible to tell where the ground ends and the sky begins. All features of the landscape are hidden and you are enclosed in a totally white world.

This is a *whiteout* and the only thing you can do is to remain where you are. Driving is impossible because you can no longer see the road ahead of you and will quickly wander off it, and if you try to walk you will become utterly disoriented. Pilots learning to fly in cloud, which encloses them in featureless whiteness in just the same way as a blizzard, are taught to rely wholly on their instruments. If they try to orient themselves by looking outside it will not be long before they imagine their plane is banking steeply, turning, climbing, descending, or even upside down, and when they try to correct for these false sensations they will crash. People who try to walk through a severe blizzard do not risk becoming disoriented, they do become disoriented. It is inevitable.

It is possible to orient ourselves using other senses, of course. Those of us who do not see well, or at all, depend on touch and hearing. In a blizzard, hearing does not work either. A blizzard surrounds you with "white noise." The snow muffles sounds and the howling of the wind, coming from all directions, drowns all other noises. The sense of touch remains, but is useful only if you already have a very good idea of where you are.

Many nonhumans find their way about by scent. Dogs, for example, seem to carry in their heads a map of their surroundings based mainly on odors they, but not we, can detect and they explore their surroundings with their noses, rather than their eyes and ears. Snow buries scents, however, so even a dog cannot find its way home through a blizzard.

If you are caught outdoors in a blizzard, stay where you are. Do not go looking for shelter, but if you can see somewhere to shelter from the wind go there. Otherwise dig a cave in the snow and shelter in it until conditions improve. If you are in a car, stay with it. You will remain warmer in the car than you would outside and when the rescue parties come searching, a car on a road is much easier to find than a person alone in open country.

Blizzards of the past

Every winter brings blizzards to some places, although some years are worse than others and blizzards are not always confined to winter. In 1989, at least 67 people died in western China in blizzards that occurred in June and July, and in 1995 blizzards on the Qinghai (Tsinghai) plateau in the northwest of the country began in October. By early February 1996 they had injured nearly 40,000 people and 42 people had died.

Figure 36: *Street scene in New York City after the famous blizzard of 1888.* (Courtesy of the New-York Historical Society)

Nor are blizzards confined to middle and high latitudes, although that is where they are most likely. Blizzards killed 47 people in the area around Alayh, Lebanon, between February 18 and 22, 1983. Many of the victims were trapped in their cars and froze. In 1992 it was the turn of southern Turkey. The storms lasted from February 1 to 7 and triggered snowslides and avalanches that claimed 201 lives.

There are mild winters and harsh winters, but for the United States the winter of 1888 may be the worst ever recorded. The winter promised to be mild, at least until Christmas. It was in January that cold air pushed over the Rockies, bringing a cold wave (see page 95) that engulfed Montana, the Dakotas, and Minnesota. From January 11 to 13 gales, blowing snow, and bitter cold brought these states the most severe blizzards they had ever known. Then there was a lull, but before long the winter returned with a vengeance. From March 11 to 13 snow driven by winds gusting to 70 MPH struck the eastern states from Chesapeake Bay to Maine. Temperatures fell close to zero Fahrenheit, so the wind chill effect (see page 104) was probably equivalent to around -70° F. The East River froze and people walked between Manhattan and Brooklyn. An average of 40 inches of snow fell over southeastern New York and southern New England. There were snowdrifts almost 30 feet deep in Herald Square in Manhattan, and all roads and railroads were blocked. Fanned by the gales, fires raged intensely and unchecked because fire engines could not reach them. That blizzard killed more than 400 people, 200 of them in New York City. Wildlife and farm animals suffered even more. Tens of thousands of birds died frozen to trees and many cattle died, some of them frozen solid where they stood.

This was a spring blizzard, to which North America is especially prone. In the southeastern United States, where spring arrives early, between February 8 and 11, 1973, severe storms brought more than 16 inches of snow to parts of Georgia and the Carolinas. About 23 inches fell in Macon, Georgia. Another spring blizzard, in March 1977, blocked 100 miles of interstate highway in South Dakota and killed nine people in Colorado, four in Nebraska, and two in Kansas, and on March 2, 1980, at least 36 people died in a blizzard that affected the Carolinas, Ohio, Missouri, Tennessee, Pennsylvania, Kentucky, Virginia, Maryland, and Florida. The northern states suffered spring blizzards on April 6, 1982.

Figure 37: *A severe, sustained cold spell is capable of freezing the mighty Niagara Falls, seen here as it looked in 1875.* (Courtesy of the New-York Historical Society)

In 1993 a blizzard comparable to the 1888 storm struck all of eastern North America. Between March 12 and 15 it killed an estimated 270 people in the United States, as well as four in Canada and three in Cuba, and caused at least $6 billion of damage.

Spring is a time of change. The polar front jet stream is moving north and warm, moist air from the Gulf is following it. At the same time, as temperatures start to rise and the difference between temperatures in low and high latitudes decreases, polar air masses are likely to drift south. These two different types of air meet at the polar front, which becomes very active. The warm, moist air is lifted above the cold, dry air and becomes highly unstable, and severe storms are the result. Precipitation, formed as snow because of its altitude, falls through the cold, underlying air. Snowfall is heavy and often driven by gales generated by the storms, producing blizzards.

Blizzards also occur in midwinter, of course. In 1891, blizzards starting on February 7 and lasting for several days caused many deaths in the central United States. The winter of 1977 was particularly severe. For 19 states east of the Rockies the average temperature in January and February was the lowest ever recorded, and on January 28 states of emergency were declared in New York, New Jersey, and Ohio due to blizzards and freezing. Several other states were declared disaster areas. These blizzards began a few days earlier in the Upper Ohio Valley and Lower Great Lakes region, then spread east. At Niagara the cold was so intense and continued for so long that the American Falls were completely covered by ice, and ice partly covered the larger Horseshoe Falls.

On January 28 the storm reached Buffalo, New York. It was the worst blizzard ever to strike the city. A total of 69 inches of snow fell, driven by winds gusting to 75 MPH. Snow had fallen every day for nearly six weeks prior to the storm and the blizzard added to almost 3 feet of snow that had fallen already. By the end of the 1976–77 winter, Buffalo had received 200 inches. When the blizzard arrived, visibility dropped to zero in a whiteout, drifts accumulated to 30 feet in places, and it all happened so suddenly that thousands of workers were trapped in offices, factories, and shops. Of those who set off for home, many were stopped by the drifting snow. Within four hours all transport came to a standstill and snowmobiles were used to rescue people trapped in cars and to ferry food and emergency supplies to those stranded in whatever shelter they had been able to find. Some 5,000 cars and trucks were abandoned. The storm lasted five days. That blizzard caused 29 deaths, nine of them of people trapped in their cars, but Buffalo was not alone. On February 1 blizzards caused more than 100 deaths throughout the northeastern states.

The following winter was also severe. On January 25 and 26, winds gusting to 100 MPH delivered about 31 inches of snow over Ohio, Michigan, Wisconsin, Indiana, Illinois, and Kentucky, and temperatures fell to -50° F. More than 100 people died and damage was estimated at millions of dollars. Once again, the northeastern states suffered. Between February 5 and 7, at least 60 people died when a blizzard with winds of 110 MPH, driving tides 18 feet high, brought 50 inches of snow to Rhode Island and eastern Massachusetts.

Few winters pass without some blizzards. The eastern states often experience them and they can affect a large area. On December 17, 1973, for example, blizzards and biting cold extended from Georgia to Maine, and on February 11 and 12, 1983, a blizzard delivered at least 2 feet of snow to every city in the northeastern United States. As the winter of 1983 began, new storms began as falling temperatures reached levels where the air moving east from the Pacific still held large amounts of moisture, but moisture that fell as snow. At least 56 people died on November 28 in blizzards that affected Wyoming, Colorado, South Dakota, Nebraska, Kansas, Minnesota, and Iowa.

The following year, 1984, blizzards occurred from Missouri to New York on February 28, and on January 22, 1987 there were blizzards from Florida to Maine. Others are more local. The blizzard of February 19, 1979 affected only New York and New Jersey.

It was in 1996 that the eastern states suffered what were said to be the worst snowstorms with blizzards in 70 years. They began on January 6, with thunderstorms and heavy snow, and continued intermittently for four days. The severe weather affected Alabama, Indiana, Kentucky, Maryland, Massachusetts, New Jersey, New York, North Carolina, Ohio, Pennsylvania, Rhode Island, Virginia, Washington DC, and West Virginia, and states of emergency were declared in Kentucky, Maryland, New Jersey, New York City, Pennsylvania, Virginia, and West Virginia.

The problems were due more to the volume of snow than to winds. At 25–35 MPH these produced only mild blizzards, but nevertheless the weather caused at least 23 deaths and many injuries. Roads were blocked and airports closed. In New York City, schools were closed because of snow for the first time since 1978. Icy roads also forced schools to close in Alabama. No mail was delivered in New York on January 9 and the United Nations building was closed so staff would not attempt the almost impossible journey to work.

More snow fell on January 12, causing many roofs to collapse under the weight. Ten people were injured at North Massapequa, New York, when a supermarket roof collapsed. In Massachusetts, a theater in Norwell was condemned as unsafe after its roof collapsed, and roofs also fell at the Oakdale Mall in Tewksbury and

Figure 38: *The aftermath of a big snow in New York City, 1947.* (Courtesy of the New-York Historical Society)

the Bayside Exposition Center in Boston. Other roofs sagged dangerously, causing buildings to be closed. The Potomac Mills mall at Dale City, Virginia, had to be evacuated when its roof was found to be buckling in several places.

Roofs can give way suddenly, with no warning, when the weight on them stresses beams or rafters beyond what they can tolerate. A woman was killed in Berks County, Pennsylvania, when she was struck by a falling beam from her barn roof while she and her daughter were feeding their horses. The late snow was especially dangerous because mild temperatures added rain to the snow that was already lying there, which greatly increased the weight on roofs by adding "heavier" snow.

President Clinton designated nine states as disaster areas. Despite the disruption, the 1996 storms were not the most costly winter storms known. Damage to property was estimated at $585 million. From that point of view, other winters have been worse.

Cold air in the west, moving south and then east, brings severe weather to the central states and even a fairly mild blizzard can have devastating consequences. In January 1975, snow driven by 50-MPH winds, but with subzero temperatures, caused about 50 deaths in these states. At least 10 people died in a more severe blizzard on November 21, 1979, when heavy snow driven by 70-MPH winds crossed Colorado, Nebraska, and Wyoming. Severe blizzards affected Michigan and Minnesota on November 19 and 20, 1981, Michigan, South Dakota, Iowa, Minnesota, and Wisconsin in December 1985, and the midwestern and eastern states from January 2 to 8, 1988. All of these blizzards caused deaths.

The storms that struck the western states on November 19 and 20, 1982 also triggered tornadoes, and tornadoes in Arkansas were associated with storms in the midwestern states on December 12–16, 1987. In all, 34 people died in the 1982 storms and 73 in those of 1987. Blizzards and thunderstorms that struck the western states from March 19 to 23, 1984 did not trigger tornadoes, but they killed 27 people and at least 33 people died in a blizzard in the northwestern states in November 1985.

It is the geography of North America that makes blizzards a feature of most winters. The land mass is so large that the interior experiences a continental type of climate, with extremes of summer and winter temperatures, and from time to time the movement of air over the Rockies draws cold air masses south from the Arctic. At the same time, the narrowing of the continent in the south exposes the interior to tropical air from the Gulf of Mexico. No other continent has this combination of features, but this does not mean they escape blizzards and it sometimes happens that a severe winter in North America is also severe elsewhere.

The blizzards of 1891, for example, were not confined to the eastern United States. They struck there in February, but on March 9 they reached southern England. From then until March 13, snow driven by winds that almost reached hurricane force (75 MPH) swept eastward along the English Channel. More than 60 people died on land and more than a dozen ships were destroyed and many of their crew members perished.

Britain has suffered many blizzards, but there, as elsewhere in the world, detailed information about them is slowly lost over the years. In February 1762, for example, there was a blizzard in England that lasted 18 days and caused nearly 50 deaths, and in 1674 a blizzard in the border region between England and Scotland began on March 8 and lasted 13 days, but we know no more about them than this.

More recent storms are documented more thoroughly. From January 9–12, 1982, most of Western Europe was exposed to snow driven by gales. The blizzards were most severe in the west. Wales, bordering the Irish Sea on the western side of Great Britain, was cut off completely from England by snowdrifts up to 12 feet deep that blocked all the roads. Those blizzards caused casualties, as blizzards always do, and at least 23 people died. Western Europe suffered again in 1984. That year the blizzards struck on February 7 and 13 people lost their lives.

There were several periods of very severe weather over Europe and Asia during the winter of 1995–96. In late December temperatures plummeted and there were blizzards everywhere from Britain in the west as far east as Kazakhstan and Bangladesh. More than 350 people died, many of them in Moscow.

Later, as the eastern United States recovered from the blizzards of January 1996, the storms struck Britain. Early in February most of the country suffered and parts of it were paralyzed by low temperatures and heavy snow sometimes driven by fierce winds. To add to the misery, there was freezing fog in many places. The Sellafield nuclear reprocessing plant had to close because snow blocked all the roads leading to it and about 1,000 workers were unable to get home and had to spend two nights at the plant. A state of emergency was declared in Dumfries and Galloway, in southwestern Scotland, when hundreds of motorists were trapped by the snow on local roads and when snow blocked the A74M, one of the main roads between England and Scotland in the east of the region, more than 1,000 motorists were stranded in their vehicles for 22 hours before rescuers were able to move them to emergency centers. Some of the victims had to spend most of a second night at the centers before the northbound side of the road was cleared around 4 A.M., and others were there longer, waiting for the southbound side to reopen. A train became stuck in a snowdrift in the same area and its crew and passengers had to be rescued by helicopter. All over Britain gale-force winds and snow brought down power lines, leaving tens of thousands of homes without electricity.

Hardly had the February blizzards abated before the harsh weather returned. On March 12, Scotland and England north of the Midlands were brought to a standstill again. Blizzards even closed the Scottish ski resorts and the crews of North Sea oil rigs were stranded. The helicopters which supply them were grounded by 100-MPH winds.

Blizzards are always disruptive and always dangerous. Roads and rail tracks are blocked, power and telephone lines broken, and people are stranded. Every year, at any time between fall and spring, there are severe storms somewhere and it is not only northern regions which are at risk. Places as far south as Florida and the eastern Mediterranean can be affected, often with consequences that are more serious where such conditions are unfamiliar and unexpected.

Will climate change bring fewer blizzards?

Over the last few years there have been many newspaper and TV stories telling how climates of the world are growing warmer. This change is due to the "greenhouse effect" and it happens because we are releasing into the air certain gases that absorb heat, the most important being carbon dioxide. All the estimates of rising temperatures refer to what may happen if the atmospheric concentration of carbon dioxide doubles from its present value. Obviously, if more or less carbon dioxide accumulates in the air the predicted temperature changes will be different.

It is tempting to suppose that despite all the problems such a widespread change may bring, there will be at least one consolation. Blizzards will be much rarer in a warmer world. It is not that simple, however. Climates work in a complicated way.

Most climatologists (scientists who study climates) agree there is a strong chance that over the next century average temperatures will rise. Small airborne particles, mainly of dust and sulfate, will counter part of this warming, because they reflect sunlight and cool the surface. When this effect is taken into account, the temperature rise scientists anticipate by the year 2100 is between about 2° F and 6° F. It sounds very little. Temperatures can vary more than that from one day to the next, but these are average temperatures, so they must be added to the "base" temperature from which daily temperatures deviate.

Small though the rise seems, it may have serious consequences. As the seas warm, for example, they will expand to occupy more space, because water expands when it is warmed. At the same time, glaciers will retreat, releasing some of their water into the oceans. Together, these will cause sea levels to rise, perhaps between 6 inches and 3 feet by 2100. Rising sea levels will increase erosion on some coasts and some unprotected, low-lying areas may be flooded.

The warming of which scientists warn is due to an enhanced "greenhouse effect," and their concern about it is not new. As long ago as 1827 the French mathematician Jean Baptiste Fourier suggested the temperature of the air is affected by its chemical composition, and in 1896 the Swedish chemist Svante Arrhenius calculated that if the atmospheric concentration of carbon dioxide were to double, average temperatures would rise by 2.7–8.1° F, which is not far from the increase being predicted now. He thought such an increase would be due to volcanic eruptions (see *A Chronology of Weather* for more details).

Today it is not volcanic eruptions that are seen as the problem, but carbon dioxide released when fuels containing carbon are burned. Other gases also contribute. The principal ones are methane (CH_4), nitrous oxide (N_2O), chlorofluorocarbons (CFCs), and carbon tetrachloride (CCl_4). Methane is released by bacteria from the digestive systems of cattle and sheep, and from rice fields, and also from leaking natural gas pipes. Nitrous oxide is released from some factories and automobile engines fitted with catalysts. The use of carbon tetrachloride and CFCs is being reduced, so the effect of these will be less serious in years to come, and most governments are now committed to reducing emissions of the other "greenhouse gases."

"Greenhouse" gases have an effect rather like the glass in a greenhouse, which is how they, and the "greenhouse effect" they cause, earned their names. Greenhouse glass is transparent to sunlight, but not to radiant heat. Sunlight can enter freely and warm the contents of the greenhouse. These then start to radiate heat, but this heat cannot pass through the glass. It is trapped inside. The name "greenhouse effect" is a little misleading, however, because the temperature inside a greenhouse rises mainly because warmed air cannot escape and be replaced by an inflow of cooler air.

Scientists have measured the amount of energy radiated by the Sun and can calculate the proportion of that energy that strikes the Earth. At the top of the atmosphere, it is about 0.3 calorie per square inch per minute. This is called the *solar constant*. Some of this radiation is absorbed as it passes through the atmosphere, but most reaches the surface and warms it. The warmed surface radiates its heat back into space at a rate that can also be calculated precisely. These calculations show that the average temperature at the surface should be -9° F. In fact, the average surface temperature is 59° F, and the difference between the two, of 68° F, is due to the fact that certain constituents of the air absorb some of the outgoing radiation. This is the "greenhouse effect." It is entirely natural and without it the air would be too cold to hold more than a trace of water vapor and probably there would be no liquid water at the surface anywhere; except, perhaps, near the equator, all seas and lakes would be covered in ice and many of them would be frozen solid. Life would be extremely difficult if not impossible. So the greenhouse effect is entirely beneficial in itself. It is not the greenhouse effect that is undesirable, but the enhancement of it resulting from human activities. This is why, strictly speaking, scientific predictions of climate change are based not on the greenhouse effect, but on an enhanced greenhouse effect.

The effect occurs because of the way particular molecules behave when radiation strikes them. Light and heat are both forms of electromagnetic radiation, varying only in their wavelengths. Most of the radiation we receive from the Sun is at short wavelengths (see box below). Air molecules scatter it, but they are the wrong size and shape to hold and absorb it. Outgoing radiation, on the other hand, is at very much longer wavelengths. It ranges from about 4–10 μm with a strong peak at about μm. Molecules larger than those of nitrogen and oxygen absorb radiation at these wavelengths. This makes them move faster and collide more often and more violently with other molecules. Eventually they lose their excess energy, but in doing so they warm the air.

Different molecules respond to different wavelengths. Carbon dioxide, for example, absorbs radiation at wavelengths of about 5 μm and 15–18 μm. Carbon dioxide is the most abundant of the greenhouse gases, so the effect of others is calculated as their *global warming potential* (GWP) in comparison with carbon dioxide, which is given a value of 1. On this scale, methane has a GWP of 11 (meaning it is 11 times more effective than carbon dioxide), nitrous oxide of 270, and the various CFC and related compounds values of 1,200 to 7,100. Water vapor is the most effective of all greenhouse gases, absorbing strongly in several wavebands, but the amount present in the air varies widely from place to place and time to time and is beyond our control. Fortunately, there is a "window" at 10 μm. No gases absorb at this wavelength, so outgoing radiation at the peak wavelength is not trapped.

If the world is likely to grow warmer, even if the change is very small, you might expect blizzards to become less frequent and less severe. A warming of 4° F, after all, might raise the temperature on a winter day from 37° F to 41° F. This much warming might make

The solar spectrum

Light, radiant heat, gamma rays, X rays, and radio waves are all forms of electromagnetic radiation. This radiation travels at the speed of light as waves. The various forms differ in their wavelengths, which is the distance between one wave crest and the next. The shorter the wavelength, the more energy the radiation has. A range of wavelengths is called a *spectrum*. The Sun emits electromagnetic radiation at all wavelengths, so its spectrum is wide.

Gamma rays are the most energetic form of radiation, with wavelengths of 10^{-14}–10^{-10} μm (a micron or micrometer, μm, is one-millionth of a meter, or about 0.00004 inch; 10^{-10} is 0.00000000001). Next come X rays, with wavelengths of 10^{-5}–10^{-3} μm. The Sun emits gamma and X radiation, but all of it is absorbed high in the Earth's atmosphere and none reaches the surface. Ultraviolet (UV) radiation is at wavelengths of 0.004–4 μm; the shorter wavelengths, below 0.2 μm, are absorbed in the atmosphere but longer wavelengths reach the surface.

Visible light has wavelengths of 0.4–0.7 μm, infrared radiation 0.8 μm–1 mm, microwaves 1 mm–30 cm, then radio waves with wavelengths up to 100 km (62.5 miles).

the difference between rain and snow, because snow rarely falls when the temperature is above 39° F.

Unfortunately, it is not that simple. Although most scientists can agree about the scale of the enhanced greenhouse effect, many uncertainties remain, especially when it comes to deciding how a slight overall warming may affect particular regions.

All the calculations depend on knowing how much of each gas is emitted and what happens to it, but these quantities are not easily measured. In the case of carbon dioxide, the burning of carbon-based fuel is believed to release about 7 billion tons of carbon a year, plus or minus about 0.6 billion tons, but the estimate for the amount released through the clearance of tropical forest (which releases carbon dioxide stored in spaces between soil particles and more from the burning of vegetation) is much more approximate. It is believed to be about 1.9 billion tons plus or minus 1.2 billion tons. (Carbon dioxide is measured as its carbon content, ignoring the oxygen in the CO_2.)

Nor is it certain where all the released carbon dioxide goes. Some dissolves in the oceans, some is taken up by plants, and some accumulates in the atmosphere, but around 1.2 to 2.4 billion tons (carbon equivalent) "disappear." No one knows what happens to it.

A rise in temperature will cause more water to evaporate. Water vapor is a powerful greenhouse gas, so increasing its concentration may accelerate the warming effect. Water vapor condenses, however, so the more of it the air contains the more clouds there are likely to be. Condensation releases latent heat, adding to the warming, but low-level clouds cool the surface by shading it, although high-level clouds made from ice crystals absorb radiation and warm the air. Working out just what type of clouds will form where and when is extremely difficult, but very important if predictions are to be at all reliable.

If a general warming occurs it is expected to be felt most strongly in high latitudes. Equatorial temperatures will change little. The effect will be to shift the climate belts of the world. Tropical conditions will extend into the southern parts of middle latitudes, what is now a great belt of coniferous forest across northern North America, Europe, and Asia will experience more temperate conditions, and the coniferous forests will expand into what is now tundra.

Again, there are uncertainties. Some scientists fear that any widespread melting of permafrost (soils that are permanently frozen below the surface, although the topmost layer may thaw in summer) could increase bacterial activity and release a large amount of methane. That would add to the enhanced greenhouse effect and might accelerate the warming.

Then again, what if plants were unable to tolerate their new climates? The trees of the high-latitude coniferous forest are adapted to a long winter, when the ground is frozen and liquid water is not available. If winters became shorter and wetter they might die. Eventually, they would be replaced by other trees that grow naturally farther south, but this would take time, probably a century or more, and meanwhile large areas of forest would simply die. As the dead trees decomposed, a huge quantity of carbon dioxide would be released into the air because the organisms responsible for decomposing dead vegetation feed on the carbon and obtain energy by oxidizing it to carbon dioxide. This would also accelerate the warming that killed the trees in the first place.

No one knows whether warming will proceed very gradually, so you hardly notice the change in climate, or rapidly. In either case, high-latitude warming would reduce the temperature difference between polar and tropical regions. The polar front and its associated jet stream would then lie further north than they do now. In winter they might be somewhere just to the south of the Great Lakes and across the central United States. The fiercest storms follow tracks a little to the south of the jet stream, so this might increase the risk of blizzards over much of the country, especially if increased evaporation made the air to the south moister than it is now. There is no reason to suppose there would be any diminution in the violent weather produced when warm air from the Gulf moving north meets cold air moving south, so spring blizzards would probably continue, although the southern states might escape them more often than they do now.

Combined with a general warming, a large increase in the amount of precipitation might trigger very large, and possibly sudden, effects. The last time the world grew rapidly warmer, at the end of the last ice age about 12,000 years ago, the warming went abruptly into reverse. Around 11,000 years ago extremely cold weather returned and lasted for about 1,000 years. Scientists believe this reversal was caused by changes in the circulation of ocean currents.

At the edge of the North Atlantic sea ice, very dense water sinks all the way to the ocean floor. It does so because as water freezes substances dissolved in it are squeezed out of the ice. You can perform experiment 14 in *A Chronology of Weather* to convince yourself that ice made by freezing salt water is not salty. The salt that has been removed enters adjacent water, making it saltier and, therefore, denser. Fresh water reaches its maximum density at about 39° F, but sea water is densest at about 32° F (and freezes at about 28° F). This is about the temperature of the water at the edge of the ice. The dense water sinks beneath less dense water farther from the edge of the ice and flows as a slow-moving current all the way to Antarctica, called the North Atlantic Deep Water (NADW). It is this flow that drives the circulation of ocean water. At the surface, the NADW is replaced by warmer water flowing north as the Gulf Stream and North Atlantic Drift, which washes the coast of northwest Europe with relatively warm water.

From time to time, large amounts of fresh water from Canadian rivers or less saline water from the Pacific (which is less salty than the Atlantic) flow into the Arctic Ocean and from there into the North Atlantic. The less saline water floats above the denser Atlantic water and, because it freezes at a slightly higher temperature, it extends the area of sea ice. This alters the formation of NADW and the way ocean water circulates. The North Atlantic Drift no longer reaches northwest European shores and air crossing the Atlantic is chilled by contact with ice and colder water.

Eleven thousand years ago it was the melting of the Laurentide ice sheet, covering much of North America, that released vast amounts of fresh water and plunged Europe back into almost ice-age conditions. This time it could be increased rainfall. While the world as a whole grew warmer, the climate of western Europe would become much colder.

Common sense suggests that blizzards will be rarer in a warmer world, but common sense is not always a reliable guide. Global warming might have little effect on the frequency and severity of North American blizzards and might bring many more of them to western Europe.

Forecasting blizzards

Throughout history, people have gazed at the sky and tried to predict the weather. They have studied plants and animals in search of clues and learned to recognize those signs that are often followed by certain kinds of weather. A red sky at sunset usually means the following day will be fine, for example, and when sailors see high, wispy cirrus clouds swept out into "mares' tails" they expect strong winds a few hours later. Many of these observations are preserved as rhymes. "Red sky at night, shepherd's delight," and, for the sailors, "Trace in the sky the painter's brush: The winds around you soon will rush."

Sayings such as these are often reliable, but there are not many of them, so as a forecasting method they are very limited. They work because the conditions producing the visible signs are centered a long way away, often hundreds of miles, and they are approaching. A red sunset, for example, is caused by the scattering of sunlight by dust particles so we see mainly the red and orange light. Dust means the air is dry and the dry air will probably reach us by the following morning, bringing a clear sky and fine weather.

The signs allow us to know about conditions before they arrive and that is the only way weather can be predicted. Weather forecasting is possible only if we can examine entire weather systems and air masses and do so quickly enough to predict the weather before it arrives. No one is very interested in a method that takes four hours to calculate what the weather will be like two hours ahead!

Weather systems are huge. There is nothing unusual in a low-pressure system, with its associated fronts, that covers almost all of North America, from the tip of Florida to the far north of Canada and from the Atlantic coast almost to the Rockies. Prior to 1844 there was no way a system even a fraction of this size could be studied as a whole until long after it had disappeared. Observers could record the pressure, temperature, winds, clouds, precipitation, and so forth, at the same time in many different places, so the information needed to compile an overall picture could be obtained, but then they were stuck. Their measurements and observations could be sent to a central point only at the speed of a horseback rider. Collecting all the data in one place would take days if not weeks.

What happened in 1844 was that the first telegraph line was built. It ran only between Baltimore and Washington, but it worked and it changed everything. Within two years preparations were being made to gather meteorological data from all over the United States by means of the telegraph and at the Great Exhibition, held in London in 1851, one of the exhibits was the first weather map to show readings taken simultaneously in many different places and assembled at a central point (see *A Chronology of Weather* for more details). Modern forecasting soon followed, the first daily bulletins being issued in 1869 and the first three-day forecasts in 1871, both from the Cincinnati Observatory.

Improved communications also allowed scientists to study the way weather systems work. Little by little they came to understand better not only how weather forms and moves, but what is happening inside the mass of air to make it do so.

Forecasts and meteorological studies still rely on direct observation and new technologies have added greatly to what can be observed. Thousands of surface weather stations all over the world continue to collect data at regular hourly or six-hourly intervals and transmit them to forecasting centers. Some stations report only the conditions at ground level; others launch balloons carrying instruments to take measurements in the upper atmosphere, tracking the balloons with radar to measure the wind speed and direction at different heights. Since the first was launched in 1960, space satellites have been transmitting photographs, some taken with cameras sensitive to infrared wavelengths. Between them, meteorological satellites now provide continuous observation of the entire Earth.

As they arrive at forecasting centers, the data is fed into supercomputers that display them as detailed and constantly changing weather charts that can be related to the satellite images. What forecasters see on their monitors is very detailed. They can call up three-dimensional images showing cloud, temperature, and wind to a height of about 8 miles over a particular locality and, within clouds, the regions where vertical air currents are strongest and icing is most likely. This is vital information for airlines.

Forecasts are made by several different methods. In some, experienced meteorologists use their own judgment to assess how a weather system will develop and the direction and speed of its movement. Others, based on numerical forecasting, use the laws of physics to calculate what will happen from the measurements fed into the computer. The number of calculations needed is vast and although the method was first devised in 1922, by Lewis Richardson, it did not become practicable until meteorologists had really fast computers to help (see *A Chronology of Weather* for more details).

Despite the computing and observational power at their disposal, forecasters can predict the weather for only a week or so ahead. Long-range forecasts, for weeks or months ahead, are impossible to make and may always remain impossible. This is because differences too small to be noticed magnify rapidly as a weather system develops and moves. Two systems that appear identical at one time may be entirely different from one another three weeks later. There is no way of telling in advance what they will do and weather patterns never repeat themselves precisely, although they often do so approximately. Weather is said to be *chaotic*. This does not mean it behaves in a random fashion, but only that after about a week it will have diverged from any prediction of its behavior by an amount that will make the forecast useless.

Long-range forecasts are impossible, but short-term forecasts are now fairly reliable and the shorter the forecast period the more reliable they are. If the forecasters tell you there are severe winter storms heading your way, you should believe them.

The forecasters first look for clues in the distribution of air pressure. These reveal fronts and areas of low pressure, and if the isobars surrounding a low are packed tightly together, it means pressure changes rapidly with horizontal distance. In other words, there is a steep pressure gradient, and a steep gradient indicates strong winds. So the winds are the first thing to be identified, and their actual speed can be calculated from the surface pressures. Weather systems are usually moving, and details of pressure distribution also allow forecasters to calculate their direction and speed.

Reports from weather stations tell the forecasters how much cloud and precipitation are associated with the low. Satellite images confirm this, and provide a clear picture not only of the extent of the cloud, but also of its thickness and type around the low and along fronts associated with it. Not all fronts are active, and well away from the low there may be little cloud or even none. Water droplets strongly reflect radar at wavelengths of about 10 centimeters, so radar is used to detect precipitation.

By this point the forecasters know the size of the weather system, its direction and speed of movement, the force and direction of winds around it, and the amount of precipitation it is producing. Next they need to know the type of precipitation. This will depend on the cloud type, which they have already identified, and temperatures inside the cloud and between the base of the cloud and the ground. If the temperature in the lower part of the cloud and in the air beneath the cloud is below about 39° F, precipitation will fall as snow. If the winds around the low exceed 35 MPH, that snow will arrive as a blizzard, and if light, powdery snow is already lying on the ground the wind will be strong enough to raise it.

Once the forecasters have identified severe winter weather they begin to issue warnings. In the United States these are broadcast on radio and television and also by the Weather Radio run by the National Weather Service of the National Oceanic and Atmospheric Administration (NOAA). In other parts of the world, warnings form part of the routine weather forecasts broadcast on radio and TV.

Forecasters start to issue warnings as early as they can to allow as much time as possible for people to prepare. The warnings themselves are graded and specific. A *winter weather advisory* warns of weather bad enough to cause inconvenience, especially to motorists, and possibly danger. A *frost-freeze warning* means temperatures are expected to fall below freezing in areas not expecting such cold weather. Some horticultural and garden plants may be harmed and should be protected. People living in homes without heating should check that portable heaters are working properly and that they have adequate stocks of blankets and warm clothing.

The most serious warnings are called *winter storm watch*, *winter storm warning*, and *blizzard warning*. A winter storm watch is issued a day or two before severe weather is expected to arrive in a specific area. It allows time for everyone to prepare. As the weather system draws closer, a winter storm warning is broadcast. This means the bad weather is already beginning or will arrive in a matter of hours. A blizzard warning is the most serious of all and is issued when the combination of snow and wind is likely to produce deep drifts, dangerously low wind-chill temperatures (see page 104), and visibility reduced almost to zero.

Safety

Every winter bitterly cold weather, snow storms, and blizzards cause deaths wherever in the world they occur. Of all those who die from cold, one in five is indoors at home, half are more than 60 years old, and three-quarters are men. Most of those who die outdoors are also men more than 40 years old, but only one-quarter of the deaths are of people caught in the open. About 70% are of people trapped in their cars.

Death is a serious risk, but it is not inevitable. You can survive severe winter weather, provided you are prepared. The secret of good preparation is that it begins long before the bad weather arrives and a key ingredient is information. Your chance of surviving any catastrophe increases greatly if you know what to do and do it calmly. Do not panic, because panic, too, is a killer.

A severe winter storm may hold you trapped at home for several days. Power and telephone lines may be out of action, so you may have no electricity supply and no direct contact with the outside world. It may not be this bad, of course, but this is the situation for which you should prepare and your preparations should begin as soon as you hear a winter storm watch alert. This will give you no more than a day or two, so do not waste time.

Probably you will need to shop for supplies. As you do so, tell your friends and neighbors what you are doing and why. They may not have heard the alert.

You will need lighting, heating, food and a means for cooking it, and access to information from outside. Check first that all battery-operated equipment is working and that you have spare batteries. In particular, you will need a battery-operated radio or TV and flashlights. Then check you have kerosene lamps and candles, and matches to light them.

Check that you have ample oil, wood, or coal for heating. Once the storm arrives deliveries may cease and the boiler may stop working, either because components freeze or because it relies on electrically operated thermostats or pumps. You can use camping stoves, powered by bottled gas, for essential cooking and for heating water. Have spare gas bottles available, but store them well away from where you will use the stoves.

Make sure the stoves, fireplaces, or other devices that use them are working properly and that ventilation is adequate. Inadequate ventilation can allow carbon monoxide to accumulate in the air. This gas is colorless, odorless, and it can kill.

Using these fuels creates a risk of fire. Make sure fire extinguishers are easily accessible and in working order and that smoke alarms are working. If necessary, change the batteries in the alarms. A bucket of sand (or cat litter) is useful for smothering fires. On no account pour water onto an oil or electrical fire.

You will need enough food to last for several days. Choose items that do not need to be stored in a refrigerator and, so far as possible, foods that need no cooking. Make sure you have ample supplies of food and other items for any babies in your household. Lay in a supply of high-energy foods, such as peanuts, chocolate, and dried fruit. When buying food, do not forget the needs of your household pets. A large ball of string may also prove useful.

The water supply may fail. You can store water in the bathtub. If you use bottles, allow one gallon for each person per day and store enough for three days.

If anyone in your home is taking medication, make sure you have enough. Make sure everyone knows where first aid supplies are kept.

If you have to drive during a winter storm, prepare your car or truck. Fill the tank with fuel. As well as preventing you from running out, this will stop ice from forming in the tank and fuel pipes.

Then pack a survival kit. For each person you will need a sleeping bag or blankets; food such as chocolate, candies, peanuts, or dried fruit; and a change of clothing and footwear. Your kit should also include a flashlight with spare batteries; a first aid kit; coins in case you need to use a pay phone; candles and waterproof matches; a sharp knife; a can in which you can melt snow to provide drinking water; a tow rope; booster cables (known in Britain as jump leads); a windshield scraper and brush; sand or gravel and a shovel in case your tires slip on ice; a bright red cloth and, if your vehicle has no radio antenna, a long stick; and a large, covered bucket and paper towels for sanitary use.

Before setting out, make sure you have all the maps you will need and a compass. Tell someone where you are going, the route you plan to follow and alternative routes you will take if the preferred route is blocked, and the time you expect to arrive. Do not travel alone if you can avoid it.

From the time you hear the winter storm warning, stay indoors if you are at home. Do not set out on any journey except in an emergency. If you are outdoors when you hear a blizzard warning, seek shelter at once. If you are caught outdoors in a blizzard you may die.

At home, close off rooms you are not using and stuff towels or blankets beneath the doors. This will conserve heat. Keep windows closed and cover them at night. Several layers of loose-fitting, warm clothing give better heat insulation than one layer and than tight clothing. If you feel too warm, remove a layer. Avoid perspiring. Eat regularly and drink plenty of water.

When the storm eases it will be safe to go outdoors, provided you are physically fit and take sensible precautions. Avoid overexertion. Shoveling snow is very hard work and, unless you are young and fit, shoveling too enthusiastically can cause heart attacks. Wear mittens that fit snugly around the wrists, a hat (half the heat lost from your body can be through the top of your head), an outer garment with a lined hood or alternatively earmuffs, and cover your mouth and nose to warm the air you inhale before it reaches your lungs. If you grow warm from physical exertion, remove a layer of

Figure 39: *Philadelphia woman shovels snow after a blizzard in January, 1996.* (Courtesy of Chandra Speeth)

clothing; perspiration can make your clothes damp, which will chill your body.

If anyone has to go outdoors during heavy snow or a blizzard, however briefly, attach them to a lifeline. Use the ball of string from your emergency stores and tie one end around the person's waist (do not rely on them holding the end, because they may lose it). Then pay out the string from inside the house. When visibility is reduced almost to zero people become disoriented and lost very quickly.

You may be outdoors and far from any building when the storm begins. In that case you must aim to shelter from the wind and keep dry. Use whatever material you can find to build a windbreak. If snow is deep, dig a shelter in that. If you can find anything that will burn, try to light a fire; as well as keeping you warm, it may attract attention. If you can find rocks, place them around the fire; they will absorb heat and make the fire feel hotter. While you are working, remove a layer of clothing if you start to feel warm, to avoid perspiring.

While you are sheltering, cover all exposed parts of your body. Keep your gloves or mittens on and pull your scarf over your face to cover your nose and mouth. Do not eat snow. It will lower your body temperature. You can use snow for drinking only if you melt it first.

If you are driving when the storm begins and the vehicle becomes stuck in the snow, stay where you are. On no account leave the vehicle and try to make your way to safety unless you can see your destination clearly and reach it easily. A car is much easier for rescuers to find than a person alone in the countryside, and in poor visibility you will soon be disoriented.

Make the vehicle as conspicuous as you can. Tie a red cloth to the antenna or to a long stick so it waves above the roof. Leave the inside roof light on at night and if you have a dome light, turn it on at night when the engine is running.

Run the engine for no more than 10 minutes each hour, with the heater on full. This will conserve fuel for what may be a long wait. While the engine is running, open the windows slightly to prevent carbon monoxide accumulating to dangerous levels. Before starting the engine each time, check the exhaust pipe is not blocked with snow. Otherwise, stay in the vehicle.

While you are waiting, exercise to keep warm. Clap your hands, stamp your feet, and swing your arms. Wiggle your fingers and toes as vigorously as you can. Eat and drink water regularly. You can drink melted snow, but do not eat snow. Stay awake. When you sleep, your body core temperature falls and in extreme weather this is dangerous. Listen to the radio, sing, shout, and do everything you can to avoid falling asleep, especially at night when temperatures fall even further.

Provided you stay in your vehicle and awake, and are dressed for the weather, you can survive a surprisingly long time. Remember people are searching for you. If you left details of your route, rescuers will be following it. If not, they will be combing the entire surrounding area. You are unlikely to be the only stranded driver, so help will reach you eventually.

Almost all deaths from cold could have been avoided. Prepare thoroughly and before storms or blizzards reach you. Know what to do and do it. Dress appropriately. Take care and when the wind drops, the snow stops falling, and the temperature starts to rise again, you will be none the worse for your experience.

Index

Italic numbers indicate illustrations.